ac. 925.

Belief in the Divinity of Jesus
Christ. By the Rev. Father Didon — London
Kegan Paul, Trench, Trübner & Co: N.Y.
Cin. & Chi. Benziger Bros. 1894.

The true Christian's attitude towards
science & philosophy — light cannot be contrary
to light xiv, xv.

Lec. I. "The present state of Belief
in the Divinity of Jesus Christ" is a living one.
For (a) It has the power of lasting which is recog. by
its "harmonious correlation with the essential
principles of human nature" pp 6 – 15 esp. pp. 12,
13 on the way in wh. the Incarn. satisfies the
essential demands of our nature. (b.) It has the
power⁽¹⁾ of expansion under favourable conditions e.g.
in England & U.S.A. 15 – 18: ²⁾ also of resistance
under unfavorable conditions e.g. in France 19 – 25
Conclus. 25 – 27.

Lec. II. "The Denial of the Divinity of
Jesus Christ in our Day" — 1. Its peculiarities
2. Its doctrinal basis: 3. (next Lec.) Value of its methods.
(a) Various denials described 1. Jewish in behalf Divine
unity p 32: – 2. Gnostics trying to penetrate mystery, pp 32 – 34: –
3. Arians p. 34! – 4. Mahomedans pp. 34 – 36: – 5. Socin-

BELIEF IN THE DIVINITY OF JESUS CHRIST

BELIEF IN THE DIVINITY
OF JESUS CHRIST

BY

THE REV. FATHER DIDON

OF THE ORDER OF SAINT DOMINIC

LONDON
KEGAN PAUL, TRENCH, TRÜBNER & CO., Ltd.
NEW YORK, CINCINNATI AND CHICAGO
BENZIGER BROTHERS
1894

PREFACE

MY FRIENDS,—I dedicate these lectures to you. They were not specially composed for you, but I publish them mainly for you, and to you I dedicate them with the ardent desire that you may share my hopes, my convictions, and my faith.

As a priest of Jesus Christ, nothing is nearer my heart than to reveal Him to those committed to my charge, and to aid them to become His loving and intelligent disciples, faithful in spite of trial and persecution, even unto death.

To be a disciple of Jesus Christ, is to make a free choice of Him and accept Him as a Master, to submit the reason to Him that He may enlighten it, conscience that He may direct and command it, liberty and will that He may sustain and stimulate them by His spirit, to give up our life to Him that He may model it upon his own, to place our destiny in His hands that He may accomplish it.

The disciple accepts as truth all that Jesus said and taught; he receives all that He has commanded as the law of absolute perfection, and he endeavours to do all that Jesus did, following His example as the spotless ideal of sanctity. Every human word contrary to His word is in error, every law in contradiction with His law is evil, every life in opposition with His life is corrupt. Open your hearts to the Spirit of Christ that He may become the divine principle of universal activity in you.

Call no man on earth master ; you have in the order of eternal life only one Master, Christ. No other name under heaven is given to men to save them, free them from evil, uplift them to good.

Jesus Christ remains for all humanity what He said that He was : the Way, the Truth, and the Life. Whosoever does not know Christ does not know where he himself is going, he is not on the road, he struggles in the darkness or lies inert in the shadow of death ; and he who, having known Him, forsakes Him, strays in blindness and loses eternal life.

No human science can show us our supreme destiny ; how could it clear the way for us ? No philosophy can instruct us about divine truth, and how shall it give light to the soul which hungers for God ? No created force can raise us to God, to the Infinite ; how can it give us that life of which God is the eternal nourishment ?

The disciple of Jesus Christ escapes from the fatality of that weakness against which every living soul struggles and revolts, or under the weight of which it sinks at last in sadness and despair. He is freed from the service of false masters, for he knows their radical incompetence in the domain of destiny. If God exists they are incapable, with all their science and philosophy, of translating for us His impenetrable will. But, they say, there is no God. They have never proved it, nor even weakened the unshakable testimony by which all healthy and steadfast reason demonstrates God.

The Divine Master, on the contrary, opens to the believer the way in which he must walk and into which our Master first entered ; He reveals to him the infinite truth of which He is the incarnation, and pours into his will the Holy Spirit as a source of life springing from the bosom of God.

All that was in Christ, who was substantially full of divinity, shines in His disciple ; his reason has thenceforth the only guide which does not deceive ; his conscience, the sole counsellor who does not lead astray ; his liberty, the only force which lifts him to the level of all duty and maintains him at the height of all sacrifice. The disciple of Jesus belongs no more to himself ; he makes one with Christ, and in this intimate and ineffable communion his own mind is supplanted by the mind of his Master in him.

Faith, my friends, accomplishes this prodigy ;

it creates in us the new man, the man of God, the eternal man, the man free from all slavery to matter, from all the grossness of animal life, from all the weakness and limits of reason and liberty.

This new man created by Christ is concealed under the veil of our infirmities and our sorrows ; but he grows in secret, in contact with the invisible Spirit ; those in whom he dwells know that he will appear one day full of glory when God frees him and opens His eternal kingdom to him. Hence, in this world and on this earth where he is only a sojourner, comes the indefatigable vitality of the true believer ; he has the knowledge that he carries Christ living in him, he feels himself with Him in the light, the force and the power of God. His hope is never wearied, his noble ambitions never satisfied, his power of sacrifice never exhausted or discouraged. Always assailed, never subdued : always persecuted, never vanquished ; always despised by the false wisdom of this world, yet enforcing the respect of the most malicious ; always treated as a relic of the past, yet never dying ; abiding, on the contrary, and ever growing younger in a hostile, unquiet, variable and fading world.

He will not turn to scepticism ; the sceptic is detached from his basis ; he succumbs under the weight of his own sorrow, his weakness and his nothingness ; he has committed suicide of the

mind. While the disciple of Jesus is rooted by
his heart, by his will, by his reason, by all his
being in the full faith in Him who is; he, above
all others, lives. He will not become a prey to
pessimism, nor ask himself if life is worth living.
More than any other he knows its infinite value.
This vile earth is dear and precious to him, for it
has seen the sweet light of the invisible God in the
Word made flesh. And he himself was framed
of the dust of earth that he might grow to the
height of God who has created and saved him.

What, then, do the sorrow, the misconception,
and the anguish of earthly existence matter to
him who feels quicken within him the germ of
eternal life? And for those in whom this germ
has not been sown or who have allowed it to die,
not all the pleasures, all the powers, all the
victories of this earth can ever fill the fearful void
which is the punishment of souls without faith,
without God and without hope?

In the school of such a Master, my friends, you
will not live as strangers to your time; you will
love it without flattery, for it is not exempt from
sorrow; you will judge it without bitterness, for
its faults deserve pity; you will serve it with
self-denial and hope, as the disciples of Him who
is the Saviour of all, and for whom no wound is
incurable, no progress impossible.

The majority of cultivated men are dazzled,

puffed up, intoxicated by science; it is for you to keep cool and calm. Estimate this earthly light at its real value; excellent for the understanding of matter, but powerless to know the things of the Spirit—that Spirit which is the beginning of all things, which rules all things, which animates all things; that Spirit whose breath sways all things and on whose attraction everything depends.

Science is good for this life, for time, for our earthly span; but it cannot make us live in the Infinite, in the Eternal, which is our true life.

The vain systems of philosophy—pantheism, materialism, subjectivism, idealism, positivism, scepticism—whose ephemeral reign leads astray many simple intellects who believe that frail combinations of thoughts and theories, of hypotheses and facts, can measure the Universal, the Infinite, the Absolute—these vain systems take no hold on the disciple of Christ. He judges them and cannot be judged by them, for he is above them. His reason is enfranchised by the word of his Master; he holds this word by faith, he attempts not to measure it, knowing that it is unsearchable; human systems amuse and interest him, but they do not tyrannise over him. He treats them with independence and a good-natured eclecticism, without narrowness and without enthusiasm. He knows that they are all incomplete; why should he then submit to them? He recognises in each more or less truth ; why then should he disdain their varied hues and sparkling facets ? This proud emancipation of the mind has become for every free man the first intellectual virtue of the day ; it has always been the honour of Christ's disciples.

When in this spirit of manly independence you have taken your place in the modern world, my friends, you will soon see that it is given up to hot, eager, and universal conflicts. It is not solid earth, nor even a calm sea with a rippled surface ; but rather an ocean where rapid currents meet, and whose waters boil with fury and great noise.

Everywhere is there antagonism ; between science and metaphysical philosophy, between these two lights of earth and the divine light of faith, between Church and State, between the governors and the governed, between conservatives and the partisans of progress, between the class which has and that which has not, between capital and labour, between the middle class and the workman, between nations and races, between interests and ideas.

I know that strife is the great law of the universe, and that it works more cruelly in the human kingdom than in the other kingdoms ; but I would not have you surprised nor scandalised, nor, above all, discouraged at the view of these increasing conflicts of which our time and our country show us many examples; for I know also that the strife is only a passing state which must finally resolve itself into a perfect equilibrium.

The sole and eternal antagonism is that between good and evil; all others will end in the effective harmony of opposing forces, or—if these forces are intelligent—in mutual tolerance.

The true disciple of Jesus Christ has for evil an absolute and implacable hatred; he knows no shameful compromises; he never submits; he protests. Were he alone against a world, he would keep his faith intact like those valiant soldiers whose hands still clasp the flag and who die still guarding it, wrapped in its folds.

Except in the strife with sin, he is everywhere the man of peace, faithful to the spirit of his Master who praised the peace-makers, saying of them that they should be called children of God.

He works in harmony with the great intellectual forces of the world: science, philosophy, and faith. Light cannot be contrary to light. However diverse may be its rays, they are fused in the same brightness and they come from the same sun. In opening his soul to the eternal Word he sacrifices neither science nor philosophy; he remains the man of experience who studies visible phenomena; the man of reason who scrutinises the causes which transcend experience; and, if he corrects by faith the aberrations of philosophy, if he forbids science to go beyond its limits, he knows also how to throw upon faith the lights of science and philosophy in order to render faith more human and more accessible.

You, my friends, will accomplish this work of enlightenment, each according to his own gifts, and you will disperse the darkness gathered by those narrow minds who are deceived by inferior science, or whom false systems enslave, thrown back upon themselves, powerless to see and to hear the bright and vibrating realities of the divine world.

Mingle in the same spirit of conciliation and peace with the social and political world.

The Church and the State should not be ranged in hostile camps, only endeavouring to enslave and destroy each other. The one, the Church, is indestructible by divine right ; the other, the State, is indestructible by natural right. Both were ordained by God, the Creator and the Saviour, for the progress and the salvation of man. Their domains are inseparable, although distinct and subordinate ; the one bears sway over the conscience, over the soul and its eternal destiny ; the other is limited to matter, to the external man, to his manifestations in his social environment, to his right to live there, to grow and to act, to implant himself there in truth, right, justice and peace.

The true believer endeavours to be the upright citizen of both these realms. As a submissive son of the Church, he knows how to obey all the just laws of his country, and even to submit to unjust laws; he knows how to keep the wise and honourable mean between base servility and noisy revolt. His robust faith in justice teaches him long-suffering and patience. You will not find him either among anarchists whose savage temper seeks only to destroy, nor among slaves whose cowardice and fear encourage every tyranny. He is of the race of those who resist and die rather than soil their hands by any baseness. The freed-man of God, he chooses the storms of liberty rather than the deadly calm of oppression. His faith needs freedom to live and expand; he asks it from all human powers till he obtains it. And if liberty, in spite of some imperfections, reigns in modern societies, we owe this privilege to Jesus Christ who frees men's consciences, the First-born of the free sons of God.

Defend, my friends, this conquest of Christ every time that it is menaced by any tyrant, whether popular or aristocratic, parliamentary or monarchic. Arouse yourselves at the first clink of chains. Sleep not, for this conquest is never final; it must always be defended and increased.

I will say nothing, my friends, of the antagonism of political parties. It falls into the background, is effaced and disappears before the conflict of classes, of which the sound fills the closing years of the century. Carry there also the same spirit of conciliation and of peace; reprove violence and hatred, which are always sterile and homicidal; resist selfish oppression, which is always corrupting; these are the things which provoke bloody revenges. Injustice consecrated by custom and opinion begets disorder; no society can live in peace if the rights of all are not safeguarded.

Do not imitate those whose words are high and whose action is low; those who speak or write, and do not act; those who give themselves out as censors of public morals and who act like those sinners against whom they launch their anathemas.

Are you rich? Use your fortune not only for your own good, but for the good of all; place it at the service of thinkers and workers; do not be content yourselves in the mere comfort of personal wealth, and if you cannot yourself create or act, associate yourselves with those who think and work.

The capital which belongs to you should not remain unproductive; you have not the right to keep it unused. It is a power of God, and if you restrain it, it will explode like thunder.

Have you workmen under you? Treat them like men; let not one suffer by your fault, nor his wife, nor his children; above all, let none be in want or suffer hunger.

And if strict justice did not oblige you to

b

ameliorate the lot of your workmen, charity imposes it on you as a sovereign duty. For charity is the supreme law of all the disciples of Christ,

Work, justice, charity, that is the pacific code of new societies.

Put it in practice, my friends, in order to do honour to your Master; publish it, propagate it henceforward. The curse lies on the idle, the unjust, the unfeeling. The conscience of the age is in arms against all those who do nothing and rest content in selfish opulence; against the violent who in their iniquity take advantage of the weak; against the powerful, who, able to lessen want, allow it to extend like a devouring leprosy.

And, in order to do what is right, do not wait till this peaceful code has been sanctioned by parliament and until the State renders it obligatory; you might have to wait a long time.

The need is urgent, and, moreover, conscience is enough for Christ's disciples, and your Master long ago bound your conscience.

Exterior laws lend sanction to good rather than produce it. Evil men know how to avoid them, and upright men do not wait for their promulgation to do right. Though I do not regard laws as absolutely useless, I consider them insufficient; it is not legislation which can pacify our society which is agitated by class antagonism, but justice and kindness flowing like two sacred streams over the whole of humanity. But learn that the two streams have their infinite source at the Cross on which Jesus died for righteousness' sake, the victim of eternal justice.

In so doing, you are sure to glorify Jesus Christ, your Master, to extend His kingdom, which is the kingdom of God, to work for the good of your country and of humanity ; for you will work for the progress of truth, justice and peace.

This progress is slow, hardly perceptible in our short human lives. The disciple of Jesus Christ knows neither hasty impatience nor discouragement. Let others, worn out by strife and the apparent vanity of their efforts, fall a prey to their want of faith, deny good, and despair of the future ; he who has given his full confidence to the Lord of life, knows how slowly God works, and is not astonished nor dismayed by it ; he knows that Christ has conquered evil, that the grain of mustard-seed sowed by Him in humanity increases in secret— whether man wills it or not, whether he sleeps or wakes ; and his conscience in which divine progress is fulfilled opens his eyes to perceive that which the Spirit of God has brought about in human society.

This view brings him peace and renders him strong against evil. Why should he tremble and fear since he triumphs over it every day by his Master's help ?

This is the secret of his gentle and unfailing tolerance. He does not call down the fire of heaven on the wicked, on inhospitable cities and nations; he does not root up the tares roughly in the field of the householder lest he should pull up with it the wheat also; he does not fear to be perverted, and, God helping him, he hopes to convert others. The infinite gentleness of his Master has taken hold of him, he remembers the words, " Blessed are the meek, for they shall possess the land." He dislikes all violence, for he knows that it has no hold on conscience, and that a conscience that is closed cannot be subdued. He feels that he is the son of the Father whose sun shines on the just and the unjust; he is kind to all, after the example of the Father; and if his kindness is unavailing, there remains to him at least the joy of having loved.

The world, sooner or later, will belong, as Jesus said, to the race of the Sons of God, of the pacific and tolerant. The virtue of gentleness and tolerance is such that perfidious oppressors wear them as a mask, and they always commit acts of violence and tyranny in the name of liberty.

Yet you should not give up power; acquire

it, possess it, if it were only to gain the glory of not using it.

Jesus had the infinite power of God ; it pleased Him to give us an example, to display it only in the service of man, to heal them and raise them from the dead ; He would not employ it for His own defence, for it was His divine destiny to fall a victim to His enemies.

But we who have to defend our hearths and our country in a world where peoples watch each other jealously, in the threatening attitude of wild beasts, our duty is to strive to win for our country all intellectual, moral, and material forces, that we may defend our national honour, inspire fear in the people, who menace us, defend and avenge oppressed rights, and raise an impassable barrier between Justice, holy Justice, and the sacrilegious attacks of power. The honour of the disciple of Christ is to carry the sword not as a weapon of offence and attack, but as a weapon of defence against the human beast and to reduce it, by terror if necessary, if not to submission, at least to impotence.

Be good and gentle knights, my friends, remembering your ancestors and the genius of your race, ever ready for battle against the insolent and strong, in defence of the weak, oppressed and calling for help.

As you are about to enter the life of liberty,

you must put on the armour of the militant and the strong.

The best-tempered, the most impenetrable to blows, the most triumphant against evil, is the faith in Jesus Christ. Put on, then, the armour of God, and, so protected, you need fear nothing. Your reason will remain imperturbable in the midst of the seductions of error, your conscience will not yield to cowardly compromises, and your liberty will know neither failure nor revolt.

Take your place boldly among those who act and strive.

Open your hearts to a manly and holy indignation against evil, whatever be its form, whether error, corruption, venality, violence or cunning, selfishness, hatred or luxury.

Avoid idlers and gamblers.

Let the herd rush upon pleasure, carried away by its foolish passions. Modern luxury ought not to corrupt you; it ought only to spare you the fiercer struggles for life, to emancipate your activity, and allow it to give itself to the great, the high, and the noble battle of the mind.

The Master whom you serve is the great renovator of humanity. He has broken the vicious circle in which for ages its wounds, its errors and corruptions turned. Show yourselves worthy of Him.

Appear in the first rank of true reformers and

unwearied apostles of progress. Never be satisfied. May you be devoured, as was Christ, with a
burning and unquenchable thirst for truth and
virtue, justice and charity.

Man must be always learning; learn, study,
seek, work for the extension of light; widen the
boundaries of its kingdom.

Societies are always, in some degree, oppressed
by evil and injustice. Never resign yourselves
to the reign of evil and injustice; work and
suffer, strive and agonise, that their dominion
may grow less; and since, in our democratic age,
a divine impulse carries consciences towards a
more equitable division of wealth, open your
heart and allow it to throb with the hope of the
new order in which might shall not be right, but
in which the right will govern force.

Do not listen to those who preach to you of a
life of pleasure. Young people who allow themselves to be charmed by the voice of Circe, fall
into the abyss of sensuality.

Those whom pleasure has intoxicated are incapable of the great struggles for truth and
justice. They squander their vital force and
become impoverished; the source of heroic will, of
unbounded enthusiasms, of steadfast resolution, of
holy daring, of vast hopes—the source of all these
treasures of life without which nothing great can
be done, is dried up within them.

They may attempt, and they may succeed in, poor, fragile and ephemeral enterprises; they can never do anything really great. They seek what is polished, elegant, pretty, fantastic; but they never even dream of what is strong, sublime, eternal. Their whole nature is anæmic, and so is all that comes from them—their science, their philosophy, their politics, their art, their religion even, are all stricken with languor. Their very virtues, if they have any, are those of the sick or convalescent.

I write for you, my friends, who are young, that you may be strong; and I give you the secret of all strength—resist evil in the shape of the passions. Sacrifice them, tame them by faith, and you will store up within you that holy power which the Spirit of God will guide towards all good.

You hear howling all around you the wind of incredulity, enveloping the masses in its whirl, and even drawing into it a crowd of literary and scientific men, the masters of opinion and of power. Stand calm in the tempest; your strength is not in numbers, in talent, in power, in science or human philosophy, in money, the god of faithless and decadent societies; no, your force is in Christ, who has chosen and who keeps you, in His word, wherein are all the treasures of wisdom and intellect; in His law of justice and love, without which all is given up to ruin; in His irresistible Spirit, which has seized the world, and against which nothing earthly and human can prevail.

The first disciples of the Master were few; they had, humanly speaking, neither fortune nor power, neither science nor wisdom. They prevailed by the power and the virtue of God with which Christ had clothed and armed them. And this handful of poor and ignorant men, these weaklings who were disdained as the lowest of their nation, saved humanity and overcame universal corruption.

What they did, the same Spirit by which they did it, can renew.

May this Spirit give you all hope.

The modern democratic world may be conquered as was the ancient world of paganism; be of the number of believers who seek to conquer it for the faith, who work in secret or openly for this conquest, who know that it will be brought about at the hour determined by God; for they hear in their spirit the words ever present, ever stimulating, ever encouraging, of the Master to His disciples of all time : " Fear not, little flock, it is the will of your Father that you should have the kingdom."

Even in this world, the triumph and the kingdom belong to good.

In spite of partial defeats, the victory rests

with those who know, with those who will, with those who love, with those who die.

We know, we to whom Christ has given definite teaching about humanity, about His law and His doctrine. We will, we whom faith animates and draws towards the Infinite. We love, whom God has loved even unto death, and who have been baptised in His blood poured out for love. We die, we who throughout all ages, on all shores and under all skies, give our life with Christ in witness of our fidelity and the truth of His words.

Read these pages, my friends, with your heart and your conscience. If my cold and pale word can bring to your faith any light and any energy, can clear and re-affirm it, if it can raise among you more ardent and more resolute disciples of Jesus Christ, my greatest ambition will be satisfied, and I shall have received from God, through you, a true recompense, the only one worthy of the desire of an apostle.

Fr. H. DIDON.

Arcueil, *February* 12, 1894.

CONTENTS

BELIEF IN THE DIVINITY OF JESUS CHRIST

I

THE PRESENT STATE OF THE BELIEF IN THE DIVINITY OF JESUS CHRIST.

I SHALL treat, during this Lent, of the Divinity of Jesus Christ, or rather of the belief in the Divinity of Jesus Christ.

This belief is one of the most remarkable facts, the most prodigious phenomenon, of psychology and history.

It is the centre of Christian dogma, the life of a multitude of believers, for it is professed by four hundred millions of human beings on the surface of the globe. It is the life-giving principle of modern civilisation, the impregnable fortress which defends morals and culture, the corner-stone of that great pyramid raised by God in the midst of time and on the moving sands of humanity—the Catholic Church.

Now, at this day, where is this belief, this divine faith ? Of what attacks is it the object ? on what proofs does it lean ? what are its effects on the inner conscience and on the public life of humanity ? what is its future and what may we expect from it ? Must we abandom it as a shaken cliff which crumbles under our footsteps, or shall we cling to it as an immovable rock which cannot be submerged, and remains as a supreme refuge in case of storm, of cataclysms, of earthquake and of deluge.

These questions are to be the subject of our Lenten lectures.

You see that we shall take our stand on dogma, great Catholic dogma; but I am bound to say, even while I insist on the strictest dogma and the most Evangelical morality, even when I confine myself to the most ethereal regions of Faith, it will be impossible for me not in some degree to trouble your minds. For I cannot treat these problems as a preacher without touching into the very quick of the religious question, and I cannot touch it without stirring your souls and awakening your consciences.

The religious question is mixed up with all our political and social strifes, all our interior divisions ; it is like a flame which the least breath can revive and fan, and it infallibly provokes both enthusiasm and hatred.

Formerly, when I was young and when I felt my claws growing, I was taught to use them in order to get rid of indifference of opinion, and now I have to moderate the ardour of opinion and its susceptibilities. It is a new art and a difficult, for there is more danger in moderating a fire than in kindling it.

Those who practised the old tactics will know henceforth that the pursuit of good demands new methods; but no obstacle, no labour ought to stop the preacher who knows how to join the simplicity of the dove with the wisdom of the serpent. When sent by his Master as a lamb among wolves, he must not be afraid; sooner or later the gentleness of God gets the better of the violence of men. No longer do the wolves subdue the lambs, but the lambs transform the wolves —the world is changed.

Thus armed by Him who gives us power to break every obstacle, and gentleness to transform each into a fulcrum—this is the better way— we will endeavour to accomplish our task, whatever it be, with complete self-denial, sure that we shall conquer if only we remain faithful.

Is the belief in the Divinity of Jesus Christ living or dead? is it declining or advancing? Has it finished the phase of its evolution or does it describe a trajectory of which the term is infinite?

These questions are all the more interesting that we live in a time when, among those who consider themselves the chosen sons of literature, philosophy and the higher science, it has been, and it still is, the fashion to declare that dogmas are vanishing, that faith has received its death-blow, that it is in its last agony, that its disappearance is a matter of years, it may be of centuries, but in any case a matter of time, and that emancipated reason and positive science will take charge of its obsequies.

What are we to think of these prophets of woe with their mournful, disdainful and insolent prophecies? I ask all believers—I ask you especially who have not the simple, tender faith of children and women, but a masculine and reasoned faith, you, intelligent Christians initiated into the science, philosophy and literature of the day, you, militant Christians who strive and suffer for the defence and triumph of Faith.

My own profound conviction is that at this day, in the civilised world, in Europe, and especially in France, in spite of all attacks, belief in Jesus Christ, the Son of God made Man, remains endowed with indomitable vitality. We are alive, we are the progressives, we who believe in Jesus Christ. They who prophesy our ruin, decay and die.

I wish to prove this above all to the unbelievers

who hear me. If they have done me the honour
to come here, they are certainly not only drawn
by a feeling of curiosity, but by the desire of
hearing a word superior to the word of man—the
Word of God. For whatever man may be, he
will never attempt with a light heart to shake the
human conscience, if a superior force and impulse,
a divine vocation, do not constrain him, and if the
Spirit of God do not put the word into his lips.
Would that I might discourage and disarm
aggressive incredulity by showing how vain are
all attacks against a faith which does not yield,
rather springs up stronger and more active after
every blow.

I would develop in believers a reasoned conviction of the indomitable vitality of their belief—I
would redouble their courage; and certainly more
than any others they have need to be brave, for
in this age of incredulity and scepticism, no one
is assailed with more fury than God, Jesus Christ
and the Church; but let them know that so also
no one is more able to resist attack and despise
blows than that sacred battalion which is the
body-guard of God, Jesus Christ and His
Church.

Here, then, in a few words, is my answer to the
question. A belief or a faith attests its vitality
by two signs—its power of lasting, and its vigour
for expansion and resistance.

Whenever a living being shows signs of lasting you can say of it, "It is a strong thing and a vigorous." Whenever you see a living being manifest in its own sphere a power of expansion and advance, say boldly: "The soul of this being is riveted to the body."

Now, belief in Jesus Christ is endowed with the greatest power of lasting and the greatest power of expansion and resistance; therefore when I shall have demonstrated these two propositions I may draw the conclusion that the Christian faith is truly living, and that if believers may rejoice, aggressors must renounce all hope of destroying it.

The lasting force of a belief is recognised by one certain phenomenon : its harmonious correlation with the essential principles of human nature ; for human nature, like all nature, being immutable in its essence, it is evident that if a belief corresponds to its essential elements and its indestructible hopes, it will participate in the immutability of that nature. We ask, then, what is human nature ? What are its essential elements and its living constituent and characteristic forces ?

Human nature has its indomitable aspirations which put its energies in movement. The weight of our body attracts us to the earth and knits us to it by close relations and an indestructible

affinity. The strictest spiritual doctrine will never
be able to suppress either these relations or that
affinity, for they constitute the very essence of our
earthly life.   Earth claims us in some measure—
it is the lower part of our being.   It belongs to us
even more than we belong to it, and yet we are
condemned to seek in it that which strengthens
our body and to beg from it in order that we may
live.

Our attraction to those who are like ourselves is
equally indestructible.

Whatever be our spiritual tendencies, whatever
attraction lies for contemplative minds in medita-
tion and solitude, man will never cease to obey
his social instincts, the need of grouping his like
around him, of founding families, civilisations,
peoples and races.

An aspiration greater than the two others,
and not less essential, raises us above ourselves.

Man is an intelligent being, and as such he
necessarily seeks to know the cause of phenomena,
to discover the essence and the reason of things.
He goes from phenomenon to phenomenon, from
cause to cause, ever mounting higher, drawn
towards supreme truth by that insatiable curiosity
which is the witness at once to infinite need and
infinite power, to be satisfied only in Him whom
the great philosophers of Greece called, now

"Him who is," now "The Pure Act," now the
"Cause of Causes."

Now we say the "Beyond," the "Ideal,"
"Logic," "Number," "Law," colourless words, sure
indications of distrustful and languishing thought.
What! number! logic! transcendent logic—as the
Germans would have said fifty years ago—sovereign law. What is a law without a law-giver?
An ideal! What is an ideal without a reality? A
name, a figment of the brain. But then how can
the intellect be set in motion by that which has
no reality?

No, man is drawn towards first truth, sub-
stantial truth, which is identical with Being.
Let us say it plainly: man is drawn towards
God.

Just as by his intellect he aspires after truth,
by his will he cries after good. To be more
comprehensible to the people, let us say that
man desires happiness. That is to say, the good
which satisfies blesses; and he seeks it with a sort
of frenzy.

This force is one of the great levers of modern
civilisation. Never perhaps has happiness, so
often confounded with comfort, more deeply
stirred the human soul and kindled its desire.

Take science: it is moved by the hunger and
thirst after comfort and happiness, when by its
researches and bold invention it endeavours to

make a ray of better light beam upon you, when armed with its magic sceptre it dreams of embellishing our earth more and more, so as to give it an eternal spring and make us find in it again the paradise we have lost. But even in this eager search for comfort, science seeks for God, and man desires God.

Now the man of science may adorn my house, and endeavour to transform earth into a paradise; but such a paradise can only be framed of created, that is to say, of finite things. These cannot suffice us; the thirst for happiness which consumes us is a thirst which nothing can slake but God, the Being absolutely perfect, eternal, unchangeable, and infinite. The more our horizons extend under the brightness of scientific discovery, the more are we consumed by this thirst.

Savages are content with anything; with a little palm wine and a few fruits ripened in their burning sun; but civilised men are more exacting. Even when earth is embellished and transformed, it remains a prison from which we must needs escape; man's thirst is slaked by happiness, he cries after it, he wishes for it without measure; but that for which he is ever seeking is infinite happiness.

Another of our hopes will show us what we are.

Man is oppressed by evil; let us say by

injustice; for evil—I take a definition not meta-physical, but popular and accessible to the merest child—evil is injustice. We are drawn towards primary truth not only by our intellect, not only by our will and our sensations towards happiness, but in so far as we are free and oppressed by evil, we thirst for deliverance and hunger for justice. From this point of view I render true praise to the present age which more than any other is a prey to this devouring hunger and thirst.

Thus I can hold out my hand to more than one unbeliever who hears me, even to Socialists, and say to them : " Just as science is urged onward by the desire for well-being and happiness which we ask it to produce, so humanity which suffers, which is oppressed by evil, is moved by injustice and cries with a piercing accent, Who will show me any good ? "

But just as there is a counterfeit of true happiness in material happiness, there is a counterfeit of justice in brute equality. Our country is at this day the victim of this coarse confusion—at every price and with all its power it will have justice, and it is at the same time devoured by a passion for equality. There are those who declare this to be a crime. " You Frenchmen," they say, " are never moderate, you have a rage for equality."

This is true and must be recognised, and he who

declares it false, lies. We are a race demanding equality: the passion for equality is in our blood like a burning fire; we can only moderate the vehemence and the violence of this passion by tranquil force and the sanctity of justice.

Now, the essence of justice does not consist in giving to each man a mathematically equal part, but in giving to each man a proportional share. There is a hierarchy of rights as of beings, and this right must be respected. The rights of men and the rights of women balance each other, but the rights of the father and of the children are certainly not equal. Just so, the right of the priest, the magistrate, the ruler are not the rights of their subordinates. If we had the religious and moral sense of justice we should no more be the plaything of passions capable of setting volcanoes alight, we should be guarded by its virtue. Justice may trouble and intimidate the bad and provoke their revolt, but she is always benefi-cent to those who serve her: she is the salt of human societies which preserves them from cor-ruption.

Frenchmen, restrain your zeal for equality by zeal for justice, and you will see how many diffi-culties are levelled, how many questions are resolved or suppressed in this world where the rage for equality multiplies conflicts and lights up revolutions, while the worship of justice inspires wise laws and reduces every force to perfect harmony.

If it be established that man desires absolute truth, unlimited good, impartial and uncorruptible justice, I conclude that man is drawn towards God by the very weight of his high and immortal nature ; for the first name of God is that of Truth, substantial, essential, and supreme; His best name is that of Sovereign Good, Absolute Perfection : His most sacred name is that of Justice, perfect and substantial Justice, not only immanent but transcendant.

Such aspirations which ennoble and dominate our miserable and changing life and make man a citizen of eternity, demand an answer. Jesus alone has given this answer; and to prove this to you, I will first give you a notion of the belief in His Divinity of which you have perhaps not thought; I do not say only you who believe, but you also, above all, who do not believe.

According to the Christian and Catholic faith Jesus Christ is Very God taking manhood into Himself by the Incarnation of the Word of God in human nature. Just as we believe that God was made Man, so we believe that infinite truth put Himself into relation with us so as to answer plainly to our aspirations towards supreme truth.

Yet more, in placing Himself in relation with us by the means of that humanity to which He united Himself substantially, the Word of God has brought to us at the same time absolute perfection under a form suited to us, and with absolute perfection, the power of justice. For if God is incarnate, it is with the sole end of giving to man the truth which he seeks in vain by his faculties alone—Truth to which, were he left to himself, his spirit could never attain completely; with the sole end of giving the dominion to His holy, unspeakable, and victorious Justice in this world given over to corruption and slavery; the sole end of manifesting eternal love and eternal perfection to us in a human reality, of flesh and bone, in a reality living, palpable and sensible, and of thus revealing to us the Ideal Man, as those are willing to call Him who have studied Jesus Christ, that only Being on whose brow history has placed a glory and can only contemplate on its knees.

That is the Incarnation : the mystery of Truth, moral perfection, love and justice, which scientific Institutes disdain to-day as though its reign were over, a mystery unspeakable and touching, at which a sceptical and critical literature may smile when it hears that the divine Being in whom this mystery was accomplished was born of a Virgin's womb.

Yes, indeed, a Virgin ! for if God descended upon this earth, in this humanity, we may not think that God made Himself like the common herd.

God chose a pure and holy being—a being without spot, the Virgin; He appeared to the people, to women, to little children, to the despised and humble of this world; He appeared to all. But He concealed Himself from sceptical, proud, and disrespectful spirits, who do not know how to bow down before that which is holy and pure, whose reason is always ready to take offence and harden itself before the designs of God.

If He has appeared even for these in His infinite mercy, they have despised and insulted Him, and would have none of Him. But in spite of the rebellion, stubbornness and blindness of men, the plan of God is carried out; and to all those who receive Christ in the faith of a docile conscience Jesus shows Himself, filling them with hopes which satisfy their infinite aspirations.

And here when I speak of man, I do not mean only the modern man as he is called, nor the man of antiquity; I mean man in all times, in all countries, in all races, the abiding man; the man who is in you and in me, in all of us.

The modern man is he who brings with him the mutability of things in this changing world and their incurable nothingness, the worn-out polished man of letters, who believes in a phrase and forgets the idea, who seeks for the harmony and the ring of words rather than the harmony of thoughts; the ordinary man of science, who allows himself to be intoxicated by ideal knowledge and by the illusion of indefinite progress; the critic, who says that he can measure all reality by the standard of his brief reason rather than raise his reason to the measure of things and the heights of God. The modern man is he who allows himself to be dazzled and absorbed by this material life, whereof the impetuous whirlwind stifles and paralyses our divine aspirations.

The abiding man, on the contrary, is he who remains invariable under the mobile and restless shape of this world, who desires truth and hungers after perfection, who cries for justice and seeks it even at the peril of his life, who would give his very blood to obtain it.

The abiding man! Jesus Christ was incarnate to crown his aspirations, and it is he who in the calm of satisfied aspirations attests the perpetuity of this faith against which nothing modern will prevail, neither the modern life of the Renaissance, nor the modern life of the French Revolution, nor the modern life of the end of the nineteenth century.

The second sign by which the vitality of a belief is shown is the power of expansion or of resistance. Keep these two words in your mind, for, though they are contraries, they are inseparable.

The law which rules every living creature and consequently every belief, since every belief may be likened to a germ, is this : A creature endowed with vitality manifests itself at once by its power of expansion in favourable surroundings, and by the force of its resistance in unfavourable surroundings. This double phenomenon must be present to our minds if we would judge soundly and surely of the vitality of Christianity and of the faith in Jesus Christ which is its essence.

If it be asked in what manner, at the present day and in the modern world, the belief in the Divinity of Jesus Christ shows its vitality, I answer that to the eyes of every impartial observer this belief attests its vitality by turns or simultaneously, according to its surroundings, by the power of expansion and the power of resistance.

It may be said that the surroundings most favourable to Christian belief, and consequently to the belief in the Divinity of Jesus Christ, are those in which it has, I do not say the protection of authority, but the fulness of liberty. In modern civilisation the two countries where that liberty is largest, England and the United States, are precisely those two countries where the belief in Jesus Christ declares its vitality by its most vigorous expansion.

It is notorious indeed that in England, a country of great individual autonomy and much public liberty, where religions long respected may unfold themselves freely under the calm eye of authority—it is notorious, I say, that in England the Catholic faith, faith in Jesus Christ, is extending and developing.

In the United States this phenomenon is still more manifest, still more astonishing. That classic land of individual independence, where men are free as trees in the virgin forest, is the land of exuberant expansion. So when I chance to meet with American bishops or missionaries, I seem to see a new world where faith is living, where barriers are removed, where each has his own place in the sun and may develop without hindrance. When I see them I feel as it were intoxicated with holy independence. Well may you be happy, Americans, who have not to reckon with any one in the expansion of your living force ; and it is good to be active and to have free elbow-room, to be outside the old civilisations which have reached a point where, in their fixed and narrow grooves, men can go neither to the right nor to the left, neither forwards nor backwards, especially forwards, without finding a fence on which is written " No thoroughfare ! "

To such a civilisation I prefer the silence and liberty of the desert or of the barren plain. There, at least, I can speak to God, to Him who never betrays, and I need not fear either the

B

corrupt multitude or irritable authority, nor
opinion suspicious as the venomous serpents of
which Jesus said to His apostles, " You will
take them in your hands, and they will not kill
you "; nor the poisoned cup of which Jesus said,
" You will drink of it, and it will not hurt
you."

The American Church is happy in having her
liberty, her entire liberty, and I envy her; her
churches are built, her faithful are multiplied like
the sands of the sea; her example is a comfort
for us worn-out men of Europe, who feel
the weight of the ages. It is good to see her
vigorous youth, her power of expansion! But
fifty years ago she counted only two or three
million Catholics; to-day more than twelve
million. What an example for the unbeliever!
America is cultivated by us who believe and we
plant in the midst of this free people great trees
of faith, as in France we have planted trees of
liberty, which are indeed the same. It may be
said that the expansion of Catholicism in the
United States is due to the emigration of Catholics
from the Old World. I answer that this fact is a
new proof of the vitality of our belief, and is
an equal evidence of the fecundity of the
American soil, where faith is planted so easily
and grows with so great vigour.

Such is the lot of faith in free surroundings;

we shall see with what energetic resistance it
declares its robust vitality in unfavourable conditions.

Take, for example, our own country, France: I
may confess, for none will doubt my love for her,
that France, without being absolutely hostile to the
faith, by no means displays the great respect with
which England and the United States honour it. I
do not speak here of the question of government—
that would be to touch on politics, which I do not
intend; but putting every political question aside,
it may be said that even when the Government
shows us the most impartial and the most strict
neutrality—which is very difficult—we have not
yet the fair Anglo-Saxon or American freedom;
for neutrality is not goodwill, and without goodwill is no tolerance, no respect, no complete
liberty.

But if, leaving on one side the situation in
which we find ourselves in this country through
the attitude of Government, we consider what
results from the state of doctrines, we shall easily
recognise how uncongenial are the circumstances
in which Christian faith is condemned to live.

Consider the philosophical systems which guide
opinion—materialism, pantheism, naturalism, idealism, criticism, scepticism; fundamentally and in
various forms negation, doubt, forgetfulness of
God. If we attempt to discover the dominant

intellectual tendency in the mass of minds
we shall recognise a sort of unconscious or
reflected positivism, a vehement inclination to
hold nothing as true but those things for which
there is material evidence, positive facts and
figures, phenomena of sense, which can be seen,
touched, weighed, measured, labelled. In a
word, the more profoundly we study the reasoning of the day the more surely we shall perceive,
though sometimes concealed by false modesty, a
very marked disposition which may be called
critical individualism.

In France there are thirty-eight million people,
among whom it is impossible to say how many
thousand there are of writers, philosophers, men
of science, literary men and politicians—no
statistics give these numbers with exactness.
Now, the dominant feeling among them is the
lively sense of their individuality and the absolute
right of criticism. All consider themselves as
competent and supreme judges of everything.
Tradition has no more weight with them than the
last opinion taught at the Sorbonne, an opinion
which may be dismissed or changed from day
to day.

It is clear that this is no favourable soil for
faith. You who deny God cannot believe in the
Incarnation of God; you who are inclined by a
habit of exclusion to admit only the truths of sense

cannot believe in the invisible and the immaterial, even were it incarnate in Christ. Oh, Christ! . . . . you admit that He was man, but not that He was God; and, yielding to evidence, you give Him the fairest human names, but you deny to Him that one which He merits, that one which expresses Him in his entirety. Nor can you, who accept no testimony, even when supported by authentic documents, if it offend your private judgment, accept the Divinity of Jesus Christ attested by Himself and by the uninterrupted testimony of his disciples, from St. Peter, who confessed Him on the road to Cæsarea, down to Pope Leo XIII., who proclaims Him to the world in identical terms.

You will object, perhaps, that I refuse to private judgment the right of critical examination. I do not object to your use of reason, but I desire that you should not be the slaves of a vain system of philosophy, variable and false. I desire that the modern man should steep himself in Eternity by raising himself to the reason which does not pass away, and seek thence light for his researches and the sanction for his decisions.

When you appeal to these eternal principles you will be on the road to faith; then I shall no longer fear to see faith in the Divinity of Jesus Christ founder in my country before the tempest of pantheist, materialist and positivist doctrines,

doctrines of contemporary Sophists who have rediscovered the art of playing with all things, affirming and denying by turns, wrapping themselves up in a perfidious and shifting dilettantism for which opinion makes cowardly concessions, when it ought to assail it without mercy. He who, instead of submitting himself with docility to reason, prostitutes it in every case to find in it the theme of oratorical or literary argument is but a sophist: he dishonours and insults reason, and by his attacks on faith he overthrows and ruins reason herself.

But in this human soil, so sterile and uncongenial, I will show you what, in spite of atheistic doctrines, in spite of the positivist spirit, in spite of critical individualism blended with dilettantism, is the vitality and the force of resistance of faith in the Divinity of Jesus Christ.

You have but to look about you : there are more than forty thousand secular priests in France who obey a hundred bishops, themselves pledged to one chief, the Pope. There are forty thousand monks, a hundred and thirty thousand nuns. These are most eloquent figures which cannot be explained away; and among thirty-eight million inhabitants—I do not count simple believers, that is to say, three-quarters of the women and children—I do not speak of indifferent persons who do not practise their religion, nor of the valiant and militant believers ; I speak only of the corps set in array, monks and nuns, priests and the hierarchy.

What an army is this ! I know only two sorts of armies—those which attack and hold the field, alert and active, ready to fling themselves on all points where the needs of the strife call them ; and armies concentrated for defence, in impenetrable phalanx, firm, vigorous, invincible. Such is the great Catholic army in our land of France. It is compact in the hands of the chiefs it obeys ; it is fair to see—fairer than that of the great Jewish nation which covered the summits of Moab with its tents in line and called forth a cry of admiration from the prophet who came to curse it.

Now this army, which shows everywhere a resistance that no attack can subdue or resist, does not remain immovable, inert, with grounded arms ; these valiant legions still attest the intensity of their faith by a marvellous and apostolic zeal for the diffusion of truth, by an irresistible, indefatigable, and energetic effort of charity to communicate the benefits of this truth under all forms.

Mark well those nuns who give their lives to succour the suffering members of humanity : nothing rebuffs them ; the splendid courage of woman and the radiant love of God animates them. A man can go to shed his blood and be shot through the breast by the enemy's bullet; but women's courage is shown in staunching wounds, in undertaking the most ungrateful and repugnant tasks; in these she finds a superhuman joy, like that of a mother in nursing her sick son. She succours all who suffer—old men, forsaken children, and the homeless poor, to whose bodies and souls she ministers alike. Her pity extends to every kind of woe: she has a word for the wounded heart, for shameful poverty and bitter need, for despair in the depths of conscience; she knows how to draw a tear from those who are stifled by anguish and cannot weep. How wondrous is her art! These poor and holy women are verily miracles of Christian faith in the nineteenth century.

Therefore I am astonished and saddened that in this country, whose chivalry excites the mockery of her neighbours, the unbelievers do not rival believers in recognising and exalting these heroines, whose ambition and divine genius only desire to fly to the help of the outcast.

But the spirit of sect knows neither generosity nor justice : it is compounded of passion, of blindness and of violence. Goodness itself, if it does not bear its stamp, finds no grace in its sight. It has dared to proscribe those holy women and to say

to them : " You shall not tend the sick, because
you will bring them to confession ; I will not
give you my outcast children, because you will
make Christians of them and will nurse in them
outworn superstitions." In its eyes it is no
doubt a superstition to develop in the child its
eternal soul and to nourish the hungry with
perfectness and righteousness. Nothing better
reveals the secret, perverse, and impious intentions
of those sectaries. They attack faith in the
Divinity of Jesus Christ, they attack God himself
through the veil of the Sister of Charity.

If those who are so daring as to attack the
Pope die of it, what will be the fate of those who
have the sacrilegious boldness to attack God and
His Christ ? They will die without honour and
without hope, admired perhaps by men, but
cheerless as they quit this world, which escapes
them against their will, blaspheming the unknown
force which has flung them into life, and which
doubtless delights, they say, to behold unmoved
the torture and the death-agony of miserable
humanity.

Leave, then, these noble women, who have found
an answer to your blasphemies, to communicate
their faith and their serenity to the weak and
the outcast, the old and the sick, who are about
to go down to the grave.

Do what you will, not all your philosophy, all your literature, all your science, all your socialism can teach you how to die and enter into eternal life. One only Being can give this necessary and supreme knowledge : God, God incarnate in Jesus Christ, who was crucified to teach us the secret of sorrow and of death.

In conclusion, when a belief is in profound harmony with human nature, whose essence is ever the same; when it declares itself by an organisation that resists in unfavourable and expands in favourable surroundings—this belief has every guarantee that it will endure, and can defy all things. Such is faith in Jesus Christ. Since it has existed it has always increased. In the course of its progress and its evolution, false prophets, from the great philosophers of Imperial Rome up to those at the end of the eighteenth century and in our own age also, have never ceased to prophesy its ruin; but it has never ceased solemnly to give the lie to these speakers of oracles. Christian believers, you will not allow yourselves to be intimidated by this line of augurs and by the audacity of their lies ? Cling rather to the word of Him who has said, " The powers of the world shall not prevail against Me," and whose infallible word has been confirmed by history through all ages.

Fear nothing ; let not your faith be troubled, let your reason be reassured. Vain systems rise like mists which conceal the stars from us and obscure the sky ; but God, who guards humanity, sends, at his pleasure, great winds to sweep through space, and the night which weighed upon us is soon transformed into the full clearness of the stars.

Human doctrines of to-day will be swept away by the breath of God, and those who lift up their heads will see the stars in the clear firmament. But as for me, I want one only star, and that is the faith in the Divinity of Jesus Christ, the same yesterday and to-day, and the same for ever.

II

THE DENIAL OF THE DIVINITY OF JESUS CHRIST IN OUR DAY

We have established that the belief in the Divinity of Jesus Christ is intimately and profoundly correlated with the essential aspirations of human nature. Whence it follows that this belief ought to find the whole world on its knees; for if it be true that it answers to the higher aspirations of man, why does not man pass at a bound to Jesus Christ, the manifestation of eternal truth, the incarnation of absolute perfection in human flesh, the living and moving expression of that justice which we need in this world, where the greatest evil is the sin which oppresses and devours us.

Yet humanity is not on its knees before Jesus Christ, humanity is divided before Him. Let not this scandalise you, it would perhaps be unfortunate were it otherwise; for the fate of this divine belief is the common fate of truth, virtue, justice, beauty, and even of health. Man is made for truth, but the greatest among men pass their life in doing violence to it. Man is made for justice, but the masses revolt against it. Man is made for virtue, but, I ask, where are the virtuous ? Man by his physical nature is made for health, the secret of all force and of all well-being ; but he passes his life in poisoning and killing himself. The doctors and statisticians who hear me will not contradict me, for it is they who have formulated the frightful saying, "Man does not die, but commits suicide."

Be not, then, astonished or scandalised if to-day, as in old time, belief in the Divinity of Jesus Christ finds not only believers and disciples, but also sturdy unbelievers and furious enemies. Infidels exist, and the history of humanity since the coming of Christ is the history of a violent movement which separates into two camps and sets against each other those who believe in Him and those who believe not.

I have spoken to you of the camp of faith, of the vitality of that intrepid phalanx and the indestructibility of that belief which lies at the heart and is involved in the very nature of man. You expect, perhaps, that I should immediately give you a proof that the Divinity of Christ is strongly established, and that it has invincible methods for impressing itself on the reason. I must, however, occupy myself for a while with the unbelievers, who are, perhaps, numerous here,

Every time that I see a crowd below the pulpit I always seek out my adversaries. I wish they could disclose themselves by holding up their hands as if they were voting. In every strife it is necessary to know who are our friends and who are not, to discriminate the first from the second, to put some on the right and the others on the left if we would avoid the peril of confusion, and not run the chance of firing on our own troops in face of the adversary's army. Only in the hour of an inextricable mêlée have the combatants the right to remember that celebrated order, "Strike! strike! and God will know His own."

Therefore, before giving you proofs on which the belief in the Divinity of Jesus Christ rests, I will to-day closely study with you the different denials formulated by unbelievers. Now, as in our first lecture we examined, not the belief in general, but the present state of the belief in the Divinity of Jesus Christ, so to-day I will examine with you the present state of the denial of this divinity.

It will be enough to answer the three following questions :—

What character distinguishes contemporary denial from all those which have preceded it ?

On what doctrine does this denial rest ?

What is the value of the methods which it employs?

I think these first two questions will be enough

to fill the present lecture, and that we may well reserve the third for our next meeting.

The denials of the Divinity of Jesus Christ **I.** which have been brought forward in the course of ages may be reduced to six : the first, contemporary with Jesus Christ, is the denial by the Jews ; the second, which occupied the end of the first century, still continues, and is the Gnostic denial ; the third, also still continued, is the Arian denial, which appeared in the fourth century. Then, in the seventh century, came the denial of Islam, which is perpetuated by Mohammedanism in the midst of our European world, without, however, mingling with it. Then the Socinian denial of the seventeenth century, and lastly, the Deistic denial of the eighteenth.

We now encounter the seventh denial of the Divinity of Jesus Christ; and we may note this number. Truth is one, error is manifold and changing, and I select this characteristic as a mark of its weakness and vanity. You are not, then, so strong, you great minds, since you have so much need to change while truth remains.

We need the voice of Bossuet and his vigorous words to stigmatise these incessant changes of thought among the adversaries of the Divinity of Jesus Christ.

One thing strikes me in their successive denials :

they are ever at the mercy of the spirit of the age, always inspired and modelled by the doctrine, ethics, and interests of the moment.

1.   Thus, the first denial which occurred in the life and in the presence of Jesus Christ when He affirmed His divine Sonship, appealed to the unity of God, the fundamental doctrine of the religion of Israel. The Jews, placing themselves at the superstitious point of view of divine unity, refused to admit—in spite of the numerous and transparent allusions of the Prophets—that the inner life of God in more persons than one was compatible with the unity of His nature, and when Jesus affirmed His Divinity they never failed to answer Him as if scandalised: "Thou blasphemest! Thou makest Thyself the Son of God, equal to God: are there then more gods than one?" The blasphemy was all the more revolting in their eyes because they argued with the narrowness of all sectaries, and because death was the penalty of such blasphemy. Thus, Jesus was not condemned as a revolutionary, although modern criticism chooses to say so; the documents on this point are plain and irrefutable. He was condemned as impious and sacrilegious, for having blasphemed the unity of God as understood by the Jews, saying that He was the Son of God.

2.   The denial of the Gnostics, which was at its

height in the second and third centuries, is still
perpetuated in a timid fashion under the form of
Esoterism, whose partisans are in fact only neo-
Gnostics—Orientals who have strayed into our
Western world.

The reason is plain why the Gnostics deny the
Divinity of Jesus Christ.

Carried away by that extraordinary movement
which led all minds towards the marvellous East,
where all great things originate, the Gnostics
desired to see God—who indeed would not desire
to see God?—and in the hope of penetrating the
mystery they turned to the doctrines of Persia,
Egypt, Chaldea, Eastern India, and to the Jewish
Kabbal. This mixture of doctrines and of strange
dreams has given place to two fundamental errors,
which form the basis of all Gnosticism: dualism
and emanation. There is not a truth of Christian
dogma which has not been perverted or destroyed.

The Incarnation above all was repugnant to the
dualist gnosis, which saw in Jesus Christ only a
special eon which it called the Saviour, whom it
considered as inferior to the Supreme God, and
never would look upon as having become really
man—that is to say, united to matter, the principle
of evil.

This doctrine, which agitated the world for three
centuries, is still fermenting in the minds of men,
for the great theogonic and cosmogonic problems

against which the Gnostic East threw itself can hardly fail to excite the eager and curious reason of modern man. The false gnosis which pretends to instruct it changes its error with the ages, and those whom it leads captive, instead of accepting the words of Jesus transmitted by His apostles, deny or change them, wishing to explain them according to the needs of their own systems.

3.   After the Gnostics, in the fourth century came the Arians, who are, in a sense, their descendants. Among the subtleties in which the speculative genius of the Easterns delighted, when the doctrines relating to the Trinity excited those minds that were curious in the mysteries of the divine life, certain of them stubbornly refused to recognise the substantial equality of the Persons in the Godhead, and notably those of the Father and the Son. They would, indeed, accept Jesus Christ as the Son of God, but not as equal to the Father. Arianism has been one of the great schisms of the unity of the Church, one of the most dangerous crises of faith. Its overwhelming triumph drew from St. Jerome the historical saying: "The world woke for a moment in a sort of stupor to find itself Arian." There are, indeed, invasions more terrible than that of the Goths: the invasion of error was one of these.

4.   Then in the seventh century came the Moham-

medan denial.   Like all the others, it was the result of a momentary attraction which carried away a
period, a race, a civilisation.   Mahomet gave himself out as the great prophet of God, rendering the
Arab people fanatical by a clever mixture of faith,
lust of conquest, and tolerance of evil ; and it is
evident that Jesus Christ could not be for him
the Son of God, equal to the Father.   He considered Jesus indeed as a prophet, but inferior to
himself ; he crowned Him with flowers, but took
away His glory, and overset the throne on which
the adoration of Christians had placed Him.   If
God is God, if Mahomet is the Prophet of God,
Jesus Christ is neither God nor the great Messiah.
The proposition is simple and trenchant as the
edge of a scimitar.

Docile under the impulse of their master, their
chief and their teacher, the Mussulmans have
suppressed the Divinity of Jesus Christ, and when
Mohammedanism cast itself upon Europe it attacked chiefly those who believed in Christ.   But,
thank God, there is in the faith implanted by God
in the heart of His children not only humble
adoration but bold and defensive courage.   The
Cross was transformed into a sword.   Christians
come of a race gentle and free, but robust and
warlike ; they handle the sword, not as the
Mussulman, to impose their creed, but to resist
victoriously those who menace their faith and

insist on forcing them to choose between apostacy and slavery. If the enemy should again invade us, to subdue that humanity which Christ has touched, Christians will know how to make him feel the weight of that hammer which has reduced to dust all men who have had the audacity to dream of universal empire.

5. After the Mohammedan denial there was an interval of tranquillity, for man cannot be always at war and armistices are necessary. Then came the tempestuous blast of the Reformation. In that whirlwind, in that confusion of all errors unchained, I will point out to you the doctrine of the Socinians as the new denial of the Divinity of Jesus Christ.

These persons were called after the name of Socinus, their founder, and had, like the Jews, the fanatical worship of the Unity of God. This is a state of mind for which I can only account by the native eagerness of the reason to criticise the Word of God. After denying the Trinity they denied the Incarnation of the Second Person of the Trinity. This was logical : the very essence, the very ground of the Socinian heresy. Moreover, the Reformation, tearing away a part of Europe from the living authority of revelation, sowed the germ of religious dissolution and threw men's minds on the steep slope of denial.

At the present day you will still find, among Protestant theologians, the Socinian denial ; it is true that it is continued in another spirit and in another form, but it is always the same denial which fears not to invoke the patronage of those sacred books which, when once withdrawn from the authority of the Church, hold indeed all that fantastic interpretation can desire.

With the eighteenth century appears the 6. Deistic denial. The philosophers and the men of science of that time accepted God, His divine attributes of truth and wisdom, power and goodness, of justice and providence : but they mutilated providence, denied revelation and miracle, the positive intervention of God in humanity, and consequently the greatest work of God, the Incarnation of the Word. For them, Jesus Christ is only a man more perfect and more wise than others whom ignorant people have deified. Such is the character of rationalistic denial.

But we no longer rest there, and those who remain in the rationalism of the eighteenth century are older than we.

They recognise in us a certain youth, because, coming from great distances, there shines on us a reflected light of eternity ; but those who date from the eighteenth century date only from yesterday, a short time, and they have already grown old.

They are like those stuffs which have lost their colour and their gloss; they are rags. Who listens to-day to the Deists of the eighteenth century, and yet how much in favour they were then! Were Voltaire to return he would now be out of fashion, and were the Encyclopædists to return they would seem as out of date as their wigs.

7.   A great and terrible novelty has come upon us: we are carried away by a movement of Atheism unexampled in the history of man since the Deluge; it is by this that the contemporary denial of the Divinity of Jesus Christ is distinguished and characterised. I know not what took place before the Deluge, it may well have been something analogous; but in our time, the world—I say the world in the sense in which Jesus used the word—is carried away by an Atheistic movement of unexampled violence.

This movement consists in suppressing God everywhere—the suppression of God as the origin of things, the suppression of God in their evolution, the suppression of God in their end, the suppression of God at the origin of life, the suppression of God at the origin of species and genera, the suppression of God at the origin of man, the suppression of God in the evolution of the human race, the suppression of God in the conscience, the suppression of God in human society, the suppression of God in the soul of the child, the suppression of God in the heart of woman, the suppression of God in the law, the suppression of God in an oath—an oath, an old thing, an old rusted weapon; the suppression of God everywhere, both in the universe which we tread under our feet and in the heights to which our best aspirations would raise us.

God is refused to us, but they leave us still the ideal, the phantasmagoria of the ideal, and men who follow this movement make themselves into a Church—a Church which they raise in opposition to the ancient, great and holy Church. These men understand each other, they have a common spirit; I do not say that they have a common plot. We are not simple enough to believe that the spiritual affairs of the human race are determined by plots prepared in advance. The only true plots are the secret and tacit understandings of mind with mind.

This Atheistic spirit carries away a certain number of individuals, as in the ocean a whirlwind scatters both great ships and little fishing-smacks.

This new Church has its pontiffs consecrated by opinion. It has its lay priests, its lay professors and preachers; it has its directors if you wish for another word, its men of action, its apostles—a complete organisation. And in our country, as I

said, between men who believe in the Divinity of
Jesus Christ and those who deny it the opposition is ardent, invincible, irreconcilable.

This lay Church—I stick to the word—has not
lived in the catacombs; no, it never knew them;
the catacombs are our property, our honourable
privilege as becomes martyrs. But it has had its
hours of sorrow in which it has asked for a little
liberty for all, and it has obtained it. This
Church has a stubborn perseverance, and now that
it has obtained its liberty it asks for authority—I
would even say exclusive authority. It is possible
that it may obtain it, and then woe to those who
are not in that Church and who would defend
their faith and their rights; they will have some
terrible days.

The denial of the Divinity of Jesus Christ
rests on this Church; it is only one result of
the epidemic of Atheism which now flourishes
among men.

But as God holds His fort in the humanity of
Christ, it is certain that, if He be not expelled
therefrom, He will retake all the countries which
have been torn from Him. Now Jesus is this
impregnable fortress. Fear not, therefore! I
told you recently how great an army is still
ranked around the Crucified. Let the denial
which is now prevalent by the fashionable triumph
of Atheism find you firm. Look your adversary

in the face, look at him without fear ; take to
you your armour, the armour of the Spirit ; stand
fast in the faith ; there are still victories to be
won !

Whatever be the men who serve a cause, whatever their talent, their genius, their number, their
vehemence and their power of fight, they must be
beaten in the end if the cause which they defend
is evil. Therefore Christians never lose hope,
because they have a conviction in the goodness of
their cause and in the sanctity of their faith.

Look to the past. There was a moment in
which they were a very small flock ; they had
against them the whole force of Jewish opinion
organised in a compact hierarchy ; they had also
against them the disdain of the great men of old
times and of all men of power, and yet the humble
disciples of the Crucified were victorious.

The talent of men who defend a cause is of
little consequence ; the cause is all. Victory will
rest in the end with Truth.

We have, then, to see whether the denial of the Ⅱ.
Divinity of Jesus Christ rests on solid foundations,
and it is that which I now have to examine.

The Atheistic movement, to which is allied the
denial of Christ as God, is concentrated in a
doctrine which declares itself to be the last word
of science and human thought. I mean the
doctrine of universal evolution without God.

This is the prevailing doctrine. Books of philosophy and science, great works of poetry and history, popular novels, all the literature of to-day is deeply impregnated with it.

In declaring what this doctrine is I shall speak with great simplicity before the general public, not an academic public, but a public worth more than this, for the academic public is bounded and restricted—yours are not. All kinds of elements are mingled here : here is intelligence, I cannot doubt it, here are culture, art and religion, here is sensibility in the heart of those women who hear me, and with sensibility those feelings which are even more clear-sighted than genius and more far-reaching than learned philosophy. There are the common people also ; and the people, in spite of prejudices, understand simple, eternal, and universal reason, which is greater and wiser than all vain systems. There are priests and monks, there are young people whose imagination is open and vivid.

The doctrine of evolution may be summed up in a few fundamental propositions which are its Credo :

Universal reality is a great and complete whole possessed and moved by immanent force.

This immanent force is so called in order to lay it down plainly that nothing exists above, nor beyond, nor outside of created reality.

It is impersonal, unconscious and blind. All the movement of things has within it its inexhaustible source. All chemical and physical energies, all natural energies are active and in conflict in this great crucible of nature. Immanent force throughout space and time disaggregates, reassembles and combines as it pleases, according to caprice, which we call law. It produces that majestic drama of which we are the witnesses and to a certain degree the actors. At a given moment you see the origin of life, immanent force manifesting itself under a new aspect. In life you find the appearance of sensation— again immanent force which reveals itself in a higher form. Then in animate life you see reason give its light, which is thought—again immanent force in evidence.

But this movement tends nowhere ; evolutionist doctrine knows no finality.

What is there at the end of this progress which continues for ever and never attains its close ? There is the thought of man ; man himself, the last step attained by evolution.

But if you search for God, there is no more a God. For you cannot call an immanent, unconscious and blind force God. You seek God in evolution and you find only fate.

In fact, fatalism, determinism, is the universal law of production.

Do not ask whither the world is tending. It rolls unconscious towards an unknown goal.

But, you will say, man remains, man with his conscience and his science.

That is the doctrine of evolution, in its great outlines, in its sum. Were I to draw up its catechism I should sum it up in these few words, and I believe the evolutionists would accept it.

Now, if by the aid of this doctrine we are to proceed to suppress the Divinity of Jesus Christ, I have a right to demand if it can be accepted by essential reason, as reason exists in every human being, before he is perverted or lessened by a system of philosophy.

Reason is a great power, a great instrument, a great faculty.

If we see anything real, the reason is, by its own essence, irresistibly driven to seek out and to know the cause. A phenomenon is produced, and we ask its cause; something appears to the eye of a child, it asks whence it comes : that is reason.

The men of old made theories, but without upsetting them. At the present day philosophers proceed in a different manner. They begin by doubting their reason, by analysing it, by decomposing it, and when they have decomposed it, it works no longer, and then they say, " There is nothing in it."

Instead of using this master faculty they give their minds to its destruction.

Yet I will ask the evolutionist doctrine if it has any respect for reason; for reason thus understood. It suppresses God, the infinite Spirit, at the origin of all things, and thenceforward it gives no further account of this origin. Movement, for instance, in matter: my reason says that it has always existed, it is inherent in matter. How can we demonstrate this?

Science is obliged to affirm that matter is inert, yet we recognise the fact that it moves. I ask you, and reason asks you, whence comes this movement.

I have always thought, and I shall reiterate it without ceasing, that movement is a property of the mind, and that movement in matter comes from a mind which transcends matter. Matter is in itself inert; if, then, it moves at all, it moves by mind. You suppress the reason of the existence of things in suppressing the mind which is superior and transcendent to matter.

You see life and thought appear and wish to explain them.

You say matter produces life; it then produces more than itself? The principle of causality rejects this; the greater cannot come from the less, nor the perfect from the imperfect. Life is more than matter, therefore matter has not produced life.

You say thought is produced by life and man is produced by the animal. This cannot be. The animal has its instinct, its fatality, its particular knowledge; but the animal has no universal cognisance, no will, no freedom.

We, however, are free, and we have the perception of universals. You cannot get from instinct that freedom which belongs to every man, you cannot get from the knowledge of particulars, which animals have, the perception of universals. I speak here in a common-sense way which will probably excite the profound disdain of all masters of philosophy. But these may be as scornful as they will; as for me, I am altogether with the people—popular in my tastes, popular in my sentiments, popular in my philosophy. I leave on one side those philosophers who cannot live outside the four walls of an institute; you will not move the world in that way. Academicians may philosophise as they please, they may be left to walk in their quiet gardens, taking care that the shock of a pebble against their feet does not interrupt their imaginings of what is beyond the grave. But the people, endowed with strong common-sense, will keep far from you, and recognise a principle which explains the origin of things and a law of evolution which explains progress. It will leave you to your dilettantism, and its powerful life will furnish new and great pages to history.

If by chance you succeed in persuading the people that its reason is but a dream, that the world is but a vast drama, conscience but a vain word, then will begin a bloody game; it will take from your laboratories the practical secrets that your science has discovered, and, armed with the terrible weapons it has found, it will frighten not only a quarter by blowing up a house on the Boulevard St. Germain, but it will terrify towns and, if need be, states, parliaments, republics, and the most solid monarchies.

This doctrine not only renders false and un-natural the original principles of things and their law of evolution, it suppresses also finality. Its partisans cannot persuade sound and simple reason, that great reason of Frenchmen which comes from the highest inspiration of the Greeks purified by the Gospel; you cannot persuade it that the movement which is lifting beings ever higher, and makes them into an increasing hierarchy, has no end in view. To tend towards an end is to go out of self; but no one can go outside self with-out being drawn, no one can be drawn unless something draws him. Men have spoken of an effort, of an interior struggle which urges onward the course of things. It is a vain subter-fuge; this effort necessarily supposes something beyond, for there can be no tendency towards nothing.

I know and I will tell you why you do not wish for finality.

It is possible to deceive simple minds by conceding to them the existence of an immanent principle, although we have still to seek how this principle becomes active; but to admit finality brings with it consequences which Atheism dreads. If there be a goal for the evolution of the universe, this goal is necessarily outside the universe and therefore it transcends all that is. It needs, therefore, only one further step to recognise God in His highest idea as the end of the universe. Atheistical evolutionists will not make this step, and they suppress in their theories all finality because that would lead them to God.

But they cannot suppress the thinking being, nor the essential laws which rule him; therefore I am always surprised to see sophists dedicate their powers to the attack on these laws, in defiance of human reason and of human conscience.

To what end is this strife? Is it for a wager? There are certain strange proceedings proper to those men who boast of their superiority, and who imagine that it is clever to go out of the beaten track which has been worn by good sense and eternal reason. Would it not be better to respect nature, instead of outraging her by propagating the diseased philosophy of the dilettanti?

Evidently the multitude does not understand your philosophy, but it may adopt your conclusions.

I do not wish to frighten those who enter upon a pathway where error may become homicide, yet it is well to look to the consequences.

As for us, we cling to the doctrine of finality, and as we admit that the universe has a transcendent principle who is God—transcendent, that is to say, containing beyond all others all the ends which creation presents to us; so also we recognise a legislator who is a living law of progressive and universal evolution, a legislator who, dealing with matter first, at its origin, produces movement, then with matter in movement produces life, and, when life has entered into certain determined conditions, produces animal nature by virtue of an act which we cannot comprehend, any more than we can comprehend the transmission of force from one being to another.

And we say with Aristotle that all beings have a desire for universal good—in other terms, for God—and that they are drawn to Him by an irresistible attraction.

We thus maintain God in the reason as an unassailable fortress, where He is guarded by the immutable principles of causality and finality.

Evolutionists are free to misunderstand eternal reason in order to follow the reason of to-day, a

variable reason which was not yesterday and which
will not be to-morrow.

But if this doctrine of evolution, which says
that it has ousted God from the universe, and
consequently from the humanity of Jesus Christ,
has against it universal reason, the denial which
is based upon it is of no avail. I have the right to
call such a denial irrational and to repudiate it in
the name of reason.

All that is contrary to true reason is inevitably
destined to sink and disappear; consequently all
those vain systems which, in order to deny the
Divinity of Jesus Christ, have openly broken with
reason, such as we have described it to be, must
expect to founder. Their momentary fashion
endures but for an hour; they will end as they
have begun, and having no past they cannot look
for a future.

Therefore, in spite of the talent of the men who
defend them, in spite of their number, in spite of
their power over opinion, we need not fear for
the fate of the cause which they attack; their
arms are made of untempered steel, and they will
fall of themselves from their failing hands.

You will ask me, doubtless, how a doctrine so
purely irrational could take such hold on opinion
as to become one of the most popular theories.
Fashion is a fugitive thing; and it is easily explained, in men and their doctrines, by the art

with which they know how to flatter the humours and prejudices of the time.

One of the needs, which trouble almost all the minds of our day, is to unite in a synthesis the daily multiplied discoveries of science. Now, the evolutionist doctrine declares that it corresponds to this general tendency, and brings the universe into unity by the law of universal development through variation.

The intelligent observations which have allowed us to study the variability of those beings which we thought were stable—the art with which science has been able to modify them, to fix and mould them at will—have driven certain ardent spirits to see, in the evolution of the universe, only a vast series of changes. This hypothesis is the fundamental idea of the evolutionist doctrine. Its grandeur and its novelty sufficiently explain why minds should be enticed by it; and how cultivated young people (for every Messiah has his prophets and his disciples) speak of evolution as of a Messiah which transforms Nature.

Now let us see both sides. Our age, dazzled by the light of science, detests and is afraid of the unseen. When we speak to it of the unseen, it turns away, as though, close at hand but in an impenetrable region, there arose a terrible reality of which it is afraid. But in the evolutionist doctrine the unseen is no more; it has suppressed what is transcendent at its origin, in the midst, and at the end of things. Space is void and mute ; the personal and living God has given place to an unconscious, blind, and fatal force, which neither speaks nor hears.

Yet more : a great number of souls at the present day have taken a dislike to God. God has been so disfigured, even sometimes by those who serve Him, and so belittled ! He has been turned into a God so insufficient—reduced to proportions so miserably human, so unworthy of the infinite—that many men, scandalised and revolted, have turned against Him and learnt to hate Him.

" Speak not of God ! " they say. " Leave me alone. Your God is an evil being, permitting all human tragedies. He is an inexorable being, who torments us, who takes away our sons and our daughters, and shows us no goal but the grave. He has created an universe where the great and primary law is the struggle for existence—where every man devours his fellows, where the weak strive against the strong, and where, naturally, the weak are victims of the strong. If that be your God, I prefer that there should be none, and think it an honour to be an Atheist ! "

That is what you will find in your books of philosophy ; that is what is sung to you by the

poets in their verses, full of blasphemy against
that God by whom our reason is revolted, our
goodness insulted, and our justice mocked.

Well, then, the evolutionist doctrine delivers
us from such a God. It says: " Young man, the
true heaven is within you, in the ideal of which
you dream. Woman, whose heart cannot bear
the idea of a God of tragedy, take comfort.
Heaven is empty ; there is, throughout space,
one only conscious being—Man ! He is the only,
the true God, but a God who is in course of
making himself; he grows greater and greater,
as the conscience of humanity develops. When
the work shall be complete, and the intellect
entire, God will be made, and then the human
being will be the master of a material universe :
he will dictate his commands, to be always obeyed,
and will be the God of the future ! "

It is by such dreams, such ambitious follies,
that vainglorious man allows himself to be se-
duced by the deceitful mirage of the evolutionist doctrine. He forgets that, were he master
of Nature, this God would still have to be master of himself—of the evil forces and the cor-
roding passions which sway him, and for which
the most advanced science has not yet found
either a curb or a remedy.

This, then, is my conclusion. There have been
many denials, in the course of centuries, of the

Divinity of Jesus Christ, the last of which is the Atheistic denial of our time. What has become of them? The Jewish denial has been overwhelmed and beaten back by the great assertion and adoration of the Divinity of Jesus Christ. The Gnostic denial in its original form has vanished, with all the subtleties of that East which, until the Western Japhet wakens it, is only a dead and desolate land. The Mussulman denial is still alive; and yet it has retired from the European world into those countries which Christian civilisation has not yet possessed, but which it will conquer in the Name of Jesus Christ the Son of God. The struggle is at hand. The Socinian denial is lost in the endless variations of Protestant doctrines; the Deistic denial is old and worn out. All those who denied have disappeared, one after the other, engulfed in that unhonoured grave wherein are buried together all those who deny Jesus Christ.

As for those who deny to-day, let me tell them that they will follow those who have preceded them; the way is open. I will venture to prophesy that as they are inspired by the same spirit, so will they follow the same path. It is the fatal accomplishment of the words spoken to Julian according to a tradition which expresses an eternal truth: "What doest thou, O Galilean?"—"I prepare thy bier."

This denial will join the others. All that is human passes away; and I am glad to insist to-day that in order to attack Jesus Christ you must attack the eternal reason of man. When a doctrine is reduced to this, that it must destroy reason in order to attack the Divinity of Him before whom we kneel, it has pronounced its own condemnation.

Reason is not destructible; it is eternal, like the essence of all things. Nothing destroys it, nothing of it is lost. Deniers may have an ephemeral fashion. We place our trust in Christ. He has made an eternal, indissoluble alliance with great human nature which He has espoused, in the strong scriptural phrase.

We thank thee, O Master, for having espoused eternal reason, against which nothing can prevail. We thank Thee that Thou hast become the inseparable ally of Man; men may betray Thee, but Man remains faithful to Thee. Strong in Thy strength, we will overcome those who, in order to deny Thee, are obliged to renounce all that is grandest, holiest and best in humanity; that which is grandest is immutable reason; that which is holiest is self-sacrificing virtue; that which is best is the indwelling God, the God in whom reason and conscience find their permanent sanction and their eternal justification.

III

THE WORTH OF THE DENIAL OF THE DIVINITY OF JESUS CHRIST IN OUR DAY.

THE belief in the Divinity of Jesus Christ is not only an interior fact having its reality in the conscience of believers and finding its public expression in the Catholic Church, it is at once a fact and a dogma : a fact entrusted to authentic books and bound in the chain of historical events of which it forms the principal link ; a dogma which is the synthesis and the foundation of the whole Creed of the Church.

The result of this is that those who deny the Divinity of Jesus Christ, faithful to their doctrine which *à priori* suppresses God everywhere, have proceeded logically to the suppression of this Divinity in the authentic documents wherein it is recorded, in the facts of history of which it occupies the centre, and lastly, in the dogmas of which it is the synthesis and the foundation.

This vast work of destruction has been, nevertheless, resolutely undertaken by our adversaries, who have brought to bear upon it considerable talent and learning, the art of expression, and of such thought as influences the men of our day— in a word almost all the gifts which Providence has given to those whom we call superior men : force of intellect, stubborn will, and cleverness. I should add that in this work, wherein the workmen are counted by thousands, the works themselves are counted by tens of thousands. At the first view this is terrible!

The country which has especially distinguished itself in this work is Germany. There are in Germany about twenty-three universities, and among these, perhaps, not three in which the Divinity of Jesus Christ is not denied, and consequently the fundamental dogma of the Gospel attacked. For more than eighty years a gigantic labour has been accomplished by professors, writers, scholars and philologists, whose aim is to eliminate the Divinity of Jesus Christ from documents, facts, and dogmas.

I regret to be obliged to recognise that in this work France is the servant of Germany. To recognise this will not influence my judgment, nor the conclusions that I have to draw; but I always remark with sorrow the inferiority of my country. Even in this work of the denial of the Divinity of Jesus Christ we have done nothing but borrow from Germany, and we are borrowing still. She extracts the ingot which we coin.

We must consider what this work is worth. Now this is the principle on which every such examination should depend. Every criticism having for its object the elimination of a document, the suppression of a fact, the negation of a dogma gains its power from the method. The legitimacy of the method guarantees the legitimacy of the operation; arbitrary or erroneous methods carry with them the unreality and the falsity of the result.

What, then, is the worth of the method of the denial of the Divinity of Jesus Christ? What is its worth in itself, in its essence, and next in its applications to dogmas, historical facts, and documents?

The answer to these two questions will be the subject of my lecture. I claim, as you have always allowed me to claim, your most serious and most kindly attention.

The method employed by Atheistic denial is called by a name which has been very much in fashion during the two last thirds of this century: that is to say, criticism.

A critic, or he who so represents himself, has a great reputation in certain circles. To

say of a man that he has not the critical spirit
is to excommunicate him from the little church
of scientific and literary men. Well and good;
but we must agree on a definition of criticism.
In its full, noble and absolute sense it is the
exercise of judgment; now, judgment being the
sovereign faculty, it is clear that a man who
is dowered with criticism in a special manner is a
sort of sovereign, while he who is deprived of it
must always remain a subject.

The act of judging consists in trying anything
by its absolute or conventional law.

When we judge, trying any given thing exactly
and impartially by an absolute law, the judgment
is full, absolute, and convincing.

When, on the contrary, it tries anything by
a conventional standard, the judgment has only
the worth of that standard; it is arbitrary, if
the standard is fantastic and capricious; it is
erroneous and absurd if the standard is false
and absurd.

You admit that a beautiful face demands a
Grecian nose : whenever you meet with a Kalmuk
nose you say there is no beauty in that face ; that
is to judge by a conventional standard.

Now, the criticism of our day which is concerned
with the Divinity of Jesus Christ cannot be re-
ferred to any standard of appreciation, judgment,
or criticism.

For a standard is either absolutely convincing to all reasonable and intelligent minds, or it is purely conventional, and therefore disputable, arbitrary or even erroneous.

The criticism of to-day has no other standard than the doctrine on which it depends—that is to say, the system of universal and necessitarian evolution, without beginning and without object. I remark, in the first place, that this system is new, and consequently very liable to fall, for in the domain of thought, whatever is new is condemned beforehand; in the order of truth whatever is new is condemned —truth was yesterday, it is to-day, it is and does not become ; it is not the same with whatever is new in the order of experience. But in the order of abstract and absolute truth there can be no discovery. We neither discovered God, nor the soul, nor the mind ; we can only seek to explain them. So Christianity, which was at the outset called a novelty, said : Christ is from all eternity, He is the principle of things, and He will be the end of things, He is the Alpha and the Omega ; and therefore He holds the centre of all things.

But the doctrine of evolution, a thing of yesterday, is only one of the variable forms, one of the aberrations of individual reason ; founded on facts which are by no means established. I admit that it is of avail for certain minds which are led astray, but in itself it is disputable ;

indeed, it relies on axioms which cannot be sustained by reason.

A doctrine which does not claim universal assent cannot be an universal standard. And when it is said that the doctrine of evolution is taught by eminent men I answer that matters nothing to me ; I refuse it in spite of them. I refuse it with a certain pride, and if you say that I am behind the age I hardly care to defend myself : for there can be no advancement or progress except on condition of respecting the essential laws of the human mind. Now, the doctrine of evolution, which has no valid principles, no law, no finality, denies these essential laws, despising eternal, impersonal reason—that reason to which I desire to appeal, the reason of the people ; because the people lasts for ever, while the middle class passes away, the aristocracy and royalty pass away, and systems of philosophy pass away. But if I have a right to repudiate the evolutionist doctrine, I have also the right to repudiate that criticism which rests upon the name of that doctrine, and to repudiate it in the name of eternal reason.

You may flatter yourselves that you are a chosen people, the first thinkers, the first writers of your time and of your country, skilled in the art of charming and leading astray an effeminate populace which follows you obediently, when its heart begins to wither. You may even invoke to chant your creed a poetry skilled in the harmony of words; you may draw with you cultured youth as they are called; but there is a power which you will not lead—the common-sense of man, the strong masses which make the people.

When you turn against God the gifts with which He has endowed you, you will not shake His reign in humanity; your partial and ephemeral triumphs will only serve to set in relief the victorious infallibility of His word and of the faith which it has inspired the souls of believers.

We now see generally what criticism is, in the name of which our faith in Christ's Divinity is *à priori* and radically denied. We have now to enter upon the details. I will be brief and elementary.

I am not delivering a course of lectures at the Sorbonne for the initiated; I am teaching eternal and simple truths which everybody can understand, because "everybody" constitutes this congregation. Yet I will give you a true idea of the great work of destruction undertaken by criticism—a sufficient idea to enable you to understand it. All who act, all who strive, need to know the adversary's tactics. A concealed enemy is difficult to conquer; brought out into the open he is half vanquished.

Why were we beaten by Germany? Because we did not know her. Why shall we be the conquerors? Because we do know her. I do not wish to be a false prophet, but it pleases me to be a prophet. Pardon me this remembrance and this momentary digression.

I come to the facts. When criticism wished to *l.* realise its destructive plan, it found itself in the presence of documents in which the Divinity of Jesus Christ is clearly affirmed on every page, in every line, almost in every word.

These documents are the Gospels, the Epistles, and the Acts of the Apostles. Now in virtue of its fundamental principle it is obliged to deny and to suppress this affirmation, which is equivalent to the suppression of the documents themselves.

This was sometimes undertaken, at least in part, at the commencement of Christianity. Certain heretics who were annoyed by a page of St. Luke unscrupulously tore it out, and so we have the mutilated Gospel of Marcion.

At the present day nothing more can be suppressed. The documents speak for themselves, they are there, and however much people might like to practise these mutilations they shrink from so rough a process. The rock is so deeply rooted in the bowels of the earth that it bears us all, and there is no pickaxe which can deal with it, no explosive capable of disintegrating it. Whether we like it or not, we must accept these documents, whose historical nature is victorious over all attacks and recognised by the most exacting. As these documents cannot be suppressed, criticism must interpret them, in order to suppress by that interpretation the Divinity of Jesus Christ contained in them. It is a laborious work, but the workmen are so persevering, have so much ability and suppleness, that, in spite of difficulties, they have applied themselves to the task with a courage and skill worthy of a better cause.

Nevertheless, in this work which they conduct so ably they have encountered a principle and a law of interpretation which sways all critics. Now this principle and this law hold them in check and refute them.

Certainly a book is in appearance nothing but a few leaves of paper, inert matter, worthless parchment, some letters written on wood, on bark, on metal, on stone, more or less well carved, which would seem to have no force.

This is a mistake. In that book there is the idea, the thought of a man. When, therefore, a document has to be interpreted, the critic finds himself in presence of a primary and inflexible law; in every interpretation he must give the idea and the thought of the authors. He must not seek for the discovery of some sense or other, nor put into the book the idea which he has in his own head; his genius should identify him with the soul of the writer.

You write a commentary on Tacitus and try to decipher those concise phrases in which sometimes the thought can scarcely be contained, so vigorous is it and so powerful the emotion ; you have not to put into it the thought of any modern man, but that of Tacitus himself ; if not, you falsify it and are a bad interpreter.

Now mark this well. Criticism which rests on the doctrine of evolution is forced, when interpreting those documents, to introduce evolutionary and atheistic thought wherever the Divinity of Jesus Christ is formulated—that is to say, in every page, in every line, in every word.

If the four Evangelists, if St. Paul, St. Peter, and St. John, sublimest of all, had been the partisans of evolutionary and atheistic doctrines, you the atheists of to-day would be the born interpreters of those authors. Therefore I willingly recognise your competence to translate Lucretius, the pantheist and naturalist ; but when I see you interpreting authors in whose conscience faith in the Divinity of Jesus Christ is as a springing well penetrating all thoughts, I cannot master my indignation, and I am tempted to tear from your profane hands those books which breathe a Divinity of which you are the living denial.

E

In order to understand a book we must possess its spirit. The dilemma is forced upon us : either you vibrate with the genius of the author and then you understand him ; or you deny and contradict, and then you can only parody, falsify, and destroy him.

There are two sorts of books : those of which the authors have ceased to exist, which have fallen into the general public stock at the mercy of each comer ; and those whose authors survive in a posterity which guards their works. Now, all human books without exception enter into the first category, for I do not know that any profane author can escape death ; I do not know that any have left descendants, heirs with a title to their genius and their thoughts, in order to transmit them to us. If such an author were living, the interpreter and the critic, however independent they might declare themselves to be, would have one rule only to follow—that of consulting him.

But that which has not happened to profane writers is true of sacred writers, and in particular of the Gospels, of the Acts of the Apostles, and of the Epistles of the first disciples of Jesus. You will notice that all these works, without exception, were produced by the most living, the most active, the best chosen members of the Church ; and, consequently, these books belong to the society which has produced them, just as the fruit belongs to the earth which has borne it.

Now, the Church has not ceased to exist, and these authors have survived in her. Pope Leo XIII. is the last link of an uninterrupted chain bound to the first Pope who was called Peter—a stone—the foundation-stone of the Church. Those authors whom a common faith groups around Peter are continued in the same living organism, of which they are an integral part, which keeps their books as its property, as its treasure, and as the chief jewel in their casket.

These books may not be wrested from the Church, nor treated simply as the works of Livy, of Horace, or of Tacitus. In the name of exegesis and of grammar, which you know better than St. Paul, for he spoke Greek very badly; in the name of history, which you know better than sacred authors and even better than certain Popes who had no special mission to study it; in the name of grammar and of history, you venture to take these books and declare that you can give me the true sense of them. I reject your claim just as the representative of a family would reject a gentleman who came to take away the deeds of his ancestral inheritance and affirmed that he could interpret his title to nobility. And were the degenerate son of ancestors whom he has forgotten obliged to have recourse to some pupil of the Heralds' College, I should have the right to say to him : " My friend, he who can no longer understand his title-deeds has no right to them."

But the Church lives on her books, she places in them all her doctrine and a large portion of her treasure : you have not the right to interpret them, I do not say against her, but without her.

I will not follow criticism into its detailed interpretations. I will restrict myself to one example, the most remarkable and the nearest to our subject, in order to explain my thought.

I choose the word " Son " of God. Jesus Christ, says the Gospel in every page, is the Son of God, and I say to a critic : " Tell me, you who are a Greek or an Arabic scholar, what that word means." He will answer me, " The expression has three senses : a metaphorical sense "—very good !—" a moral sense "—very good !—" and an absolute sense "—quite right ! In what sense am I to understand it in the Gospels ? It is plain that if the gentleman whom I am questioning is an adept in the evolutionist doctrine he will answer me: " You can only understand it in the metaphorical sense ; that is to say, in a very large sense which at bottom means nothing."

But, pardon me, the society exists to which these books belong, and since it lives on these books, since it has produced them and keeps them, since without it you would not have them at all, it seems to me that its opinion ought to have some importance, indeed that it rules and solves the question.

I ask of the Church's authority what is the sense of this word " Son " of God, and the Church answers me with a voice which has always been the same for eighteen hundred years : that this expression has to be taken in its most absolute sense—in the sense of a natural filiation, in the sense of a perfect filiation which places the Son on an equality of wisdom, power, virtue, majesty and glory with God the Father. That is the Church's sense.

Now, no interpretation whatever can prevail against this testimony. In fact, we have to find what Peter thought when he said : " Thou art the Son of God," and what Jesus Christ thought when, addressing Himself to Peter, He said : " I am the Son of God."

Now the Church gives us the sense of this word " Son " of God—the sense which she has always and will always attach to it. The interpreters may take it or leave it ; they can maintain their interpretation in the name of their criticism, but they cannot say that the thought of St. Peter was their thought ; it is what he transmitted to his successors, what the Church has guarded incorruptible through all ages as her unshaken foundation, the substance of her faith and of her dogma.

2 .   If the doctrine of those who deny Jesus Christ is powerless to alter the documents or to falsify their true sense, it will not be more successful when applied to history, whose continuous web shows the succession of phenomena. We will examine it at work.

There is that which dominates facts, since facts are only the elements of history—I mean the interpretation of facts, which we may call the philosophy of history.

The historian who respects history, and all declare and must declare that they respect it, is bound to admit the sovereignty of facts, not in opposition to the sovereignty of right, but in this sense that fact when once established is necessarily accepted.

As to the interpretation of facts, it is subject to all the variations of human thought.

None of us, however great our genius, can declare that our sight can pierce to the bottom of phenomena—a web which constitutes the fairest representation which the human eye can possibly contemplate, and which God spreads before Himself in the splendour of His eternity.

But if the sovereignty of facts exists there are two conditions under which it bears sway : the first condition is that a fact should not be contradictory, for, if it were, it would no longer be a fact, whatever a refined philosophy may think, and before this condition I disdain to pause. The second condition is that it must be attested by a witness worthy of credence.

Now, when those who deny the Divinity of Jesus Christ find themselves in presence of the facts of history related by witnesses, they have not observed this double law in virtue of which the human mind has no right to reject a fact when it is not contradictory, nor to reject evidence which affirms a fact. For the negative criticism of the Divinity of Jesus Christ in presence of facts which do not square with its preconceived system has not only rejected but suppressed them. Now mark this : this system does not admit facts outside the laws of nature and humanity ; it rests on that fundamental but arbitrary principle that there are only two factors, man and nature ; it has erased the third—God.

When, therefore, it comes in contact with historic facts which do not fall under the laws of nature and humanity it has suppressed or tried to diminish them. I will only name, to keep within my subject, miracles and prophecies. I have not here to sustain the thesis either of miracle or prophecy, but I declare that they exist, and that every time that they have been found in the way of negative criticism it has spurned them aside.

But you cannot treat with disdain the flood of miracles which substantiate the Divinity of Jesus Christ, nor those striking prophecies which fell from His holy lips. It cannot be denied that Jesus Christ broke the stone of His tomb; it cannot be denied that Jesus Christ proclaimed that the Temple should be destroyed and that stone should not remain upon stone ; it cannot be denied that He announced that His work would be known throughout the world; it cannot be denied that He foretold the dispersion of that people which misunderstood, abandoned, betrayed and condemned Him ; it cannot be denied that He prophesied His scourging and the insults which were heaped upon Him, and His death upon the cross ; it cannot be denied that, steadfast and calm, though at times troubled, He went to Calvary and died upon the cross.

Now, historians, when they have approached that figure, have immediately forgotten Him and declined to see Him. Yet this great Being, who has no human name, this Son of Man, knew that He went to death, and to that very death which He had predicted.

Neither can it be denied that He touched the sick and healed them. You interpret this, and you say it was a magnetic touch. Nothing of the sort. Magnetic touch does not raise the dead. I have seen magnetic passes, I know all about that. You take advantage of obscurity, you creep into the cave where darkness allows you to hide; but magnetism at last is known. You must find something else, and we drive you thence, perverse minds who flee the light.

You say again, nature has unknown laws, by which miracles may be explained; we shall study these laws and learn how miracles are wrought; we shall find the master-law of the powers of nature.

No! you cannot escape the dilemma; you must recognise that there is another thing than nature and determinism, than man and his liberty, and you will then declare yourself conquered; or else you will be obstinate in suppressing and falsifying doctrines full of miracles, prophecies not to be denied by any unprejudiced straightforward people, and you will be justly accused of violating history and of mutilating reality.

Then you will say: "You force us to accept what is absurd." No, because I recognise that reason has the right to refuse a fact which implies a contradiction; but neither the miracles nor the prophecies of which Christian history is woven, are in the category of absurd or contradictory facts; for if they escape the laws of humanity and of nature they enter into that higher law of God which transcends nature and humanity. Therefore I

appeal to all candid minds, to the young who have
not made an unclean alliance with doctrines as
narrow as the brains that have conceived them, and
I say : " Young people, who thirst for intellectual
liberty, recognise only one master after God—
your reason, freed from all systems, your essential
reason, popular in the full sense of the word,
dowered with principles of causality and finality ;
and with those irresistible principles triumph over
pantheism, atheism, criticism.   You are stronger
than the doctrines of a day. He who has on his side
eternal reason soars above his time, above mislead-
ing prejudices and those false theories which may
turn from the right path men less sincere, less
impatient of all servitude and of all bounds."

Since the facts of which I speak belong to the
past, they can only be know by the intermediary
of witnesses who attest them.   These witnesses
are men like to us, who are sometimes of great,
sometimes of little value ; for us who believe they
are of great value.

Now, what should be the attitude of a free and
independent man before the witnesses of history ?
and first, what is the attitude of the criticism of our
day ?   We must tear off its mask and see what is
covered by its involved and euphemistic phrases.

" Your witnesses," says criticism, " are simple
people—they knew nothing and consequently are

not worth hearing. Peter, Paul, the Magdalen, were fanatics, Jews in whom the narrowest prejudices were engrained. The natural was not then distinguished from the supernatural, nor were the scientific methods of investigation known. An academic body capable of judging learnedly about everything had not then been formed. We must see if those great personages had recognised scientifically the healings of the sick, the resurrections, the prophecies. We might then have believed them." But—but—I will translate your thought—why should we always live in this sort of masked hypocrisy? You mean this: "These witnesses are mere fools! We do not believe in fools."

Well, I for my part do not agree with those who despise man. I respect man: Peter, Paul, the Magdalen, all those who knew Jesus. I venerate them, I accept their testimony, I think that it ought to be received, because it comes from souls who were detached from self, sincere souls who told what they had seen, heroic souls who gave their life to maintain the truth. I do not call the one—I borrow the phrases from contemporary criticism—an hysterical enthusiast, and the others fanatics. I see in Magdalen the great penitent— we in this church are under her patronage; and I salute in the Apostles the conquerors of the pagan world. They are worthy of the respect due to all who have boldly borne witness to their faith in spite of difficulties; they are worthy not only to be respected as conquerors, but to be heard as those who are full of the spirit of devotion and sacrifice, the Spirit of God.

And now if criticism please to attack and treat our witnesses with contempt, I despise it in turn and, disdaining its attack, increase my respect a hundredfold.

The facts which maintain our belief in the Divinity of Jesus Christ have been declared divinely—that is to say, by the very Word of God —in sentences which constitute our dogmas. The fundamental article on which all the others rest is this: " Jesus Christ is, in the unity of a divine person, the Son of God and the Son of Man ; the Son of God equal to His Father, and the Son of Man equal to us, sin only excepted." All Christianity rests upon this dogma, and its sacred books are only its development.

Criticism has evidently sought to deprive this dogma of all divine character, since its main purpose is to suppress God everywhere. Just as, in obedience to its atheistic spirit, it has attempted to erase the divine from the documents, and to mutilate the facts of history, so has it wished to suppress dogmas. To attain this end it has thought fit to present them as simple statements having no divine reality and of purely human creation.

Now, see the irony of things! Half a century ago, Rationalism explained triumphantly how dogma had come to an end; and at the present day contemporary criticism claims to teach us how dogmas are formed.

It will be said, no doubt: "Dogmas must be formed in order that they may end."

Let us understand each other. Dogmas are not formed like philosophical or scientific theories; dogmas are the Word of God, received by the faith of man. In truth, they are developed slowly, in contact with the error which denies them; but they are one in their essence with the revealed Word which formed them once for all.

Jesus Christ, Son of God and Son of Man: we cannot get away from these two terms; all additional statements are only explanations. Peter had already spoken the word which contained, as the acorn contains the oak, the whole Christology, as the new language calls it. When God casts such a proposition into the human mind it grows like a grain which produces a hundredfold, and just as the field of wheat is contained in the grain of corn, all dogmas are enclosed in this primary word.

Yet, let us examine the method of criticism in

accounting for the formation of the dogma concerning the Divinity of Jesus Christ.

It began by erecting into a principle this fact : when a man exercises a profound influence over his fellows by his intellect, by his virtues, or by his deeds, by his power and by the terror with which he can inspire them, or by the enthusiasm which he excites, humanity—at least those who have known and loved him—feels the need of glorifying him.

We can recognise a true element in this principle, for error is never without a certain portion of truth.

In fact, when those whom we love pass away or are at a distance their moral beauty grows fairer in our eyes. We all have loved and lost those dear to us ; we have all felt after their death that they live again, idealised in our memory, their brow crowned with an aureole of beauty. This sentiment does not lead us into error : rather it raises and corrects our judgment. Nearness prevents our seeing clearly ; details obscure our sight, and the whole escapes us. At a distance you will perceive the true type in its harmonious beauty as though carved in Parian marble. It is the consolation and the privilege of death to embellish those whom we have lost, placing them in that mysterious distance where there falls on their idealised brow a ray of eternal light.

But the tendency to idealise those we have loved when they have vanished, does not go as far as formal idolatry or absolute deification. Now, it is this tendency, exaggerated to an extreme degree, that criticism must invoke to explain the origin of the dogma of the Divinity of Jesus Christ, and to take away from it, together with its divine character, all objective value.

These are their affirmations in plain terms:

Jesus Christ was a man like ourselves. His high moral worth inspired those who knew Him with so great a love, so vivid an enthusiasm, so ardent a worship, that during three centuries His fond disciples set themselves to glorify Him incessantly, till they made Him into God.

This Nazarene, a rebel against His country's laws, was regarded by His followers as a martyr. When once a martyr, He soon became the Messiah promised to the Jews; and, yearning to exalt Him, they applied to Him all that the ancient books contained in regard to the national Messiah. Then admiration, growing warmer in spite of time, saw in Him the Saviour of Humanity; endowed Him with sanctity, with every virtue and every aureole; and, finally, crowned His brow with the glory of God, gave Him divinity (not the divinity of the Gnostics, which was a half-divinity, and still allowed an inequality between Himself and God), but total and complete divinity; that is to say, boundless wisdom and love, almighty power and unfading beauty. The insatiable faith of His disciples gave to Him the fullness of the Godhead. It made Him equal to the Father, equal to Him whom the Jews considered as the terrible God, Jehovah; it recognised in Him the power to absolve from all sin; it saluted in Him the creative Word of the world, the supreme Judge of every creature, the Alpha and Omega.

Dogma thus worked itself out for three centuries; enthusiasm grew not cold, the worship working towards Godhead was always active for Jesus Christ. Such, in a word, is the evolutionist doctrine according to criticism of the dogma of the Divinity of Jesus Christ.

But it is strange there is no other example of a like fact. Sâkia-Mouni was not made a divinity; he simply became Buddha. Mahomet was not made a divinity; he remained a simple prophet. Moses the Jew was not made a divinity; there was even a fear that he should be too highly exalted by his people, and his tomb was concealed.

Yet these were powerful beings. Buddha has drawn millions of men after him; he has created new races, peoples, and civilisations.

Mahomet brought under discipline an untamed race, gave it a religion and a law, and inspired it with a fanaticism unexhausted after twelve centuries. Moses created a strange and indestructible people. I do not speak of modern great men, for criticism takes care to tell us, with a wise precaution, that those times are past, and men can no longer make their gods. Pagans created them by thousands, when they deified their emperors; but the art was exhausted in Jesus Christ.

But I would ask you to remark that there is nothing in common between the Pagan apotheosis and deification, properly so-called. The first placed the emperors in the home of the gods, while the other has identified Jesus Christ with God Himself. And I have the right to ask the cause of this difference? How comes it that, in regard to those great men, humanity went no further than apotheosis; and why, in regard to Jesus Christ, it passed all bounds, and did not stop at absolute deification? What was there in this unique Being so strange that His disciples elevated Him to a height which no man has attained, and with a persistence so great that the ages have not wearied mankind in its ardour to glorify Him? Those who are here—the great majority at least—adore Him still; and those who have ceased to adore Him are none the

F

better for it, nor more intellectual. They believe themselves more free, but have no more virtue. Unbelieving legislators who court popular favour serve their country no better, are no more eager, having rejected Jesus Christ, to fling themselves into the strife for the triumph of good!

I am astonished when I see those who reject Jesus Christ stanch the wounds of the suffering, when they ought rather to stanch their own wounds. I have an instinctive distrust of those who, having known Christ—the ideal of those who suffer, either in the heart or in the body—destroy in those poor creatures the faith in Jesus Christ, and feign to doubt the love of the faithful who have maintained the worship of what is holy.

Yet more. The adoration of the faithful for Jesus Christ as God was not progressive; from the very first hour His disciples saluted in Him, Christ, the Son of the living God. The Epistles of St. Paul, written a few years after the death of the Master, prove the matter to the full, even were there no other documents. The idea of a progressive deification is a pure romance, created by the needs of criticism.

If I admit for an instant that we have made Jesus Christ divine, and that this proposition, God made Himself Man, may be reversed and replaced by this, Out of Jesus Christ men have made a God, this is the result: Humanity in the most advanced state of civilisation, our own (we may say it without injustice to our ancestors, and without offence to truth), is nothing but a vast idolatry and an immense servitude, which every religious and free conscience is bound to resist. Christianity, which shattered paganism, has only replaced the ancient idolatry and the ancient slavery by another idolatry and another slavery. The women who sacrifice themselves in their heroism, are not the less idolaters, even when they have broken their chains to become the victorious legions of charity. When priests, led on by impetuous zeal, carry the Name of Him whom they call their God beyond our frontiers, even to the Black Continent, unlimited fields opening before them, idolatry leads them there. In short, if we are worth anything— which cannot be doubted—if charity is a power in our world, if justice is a passion, if all great virtues have ennobled humanity, it is thanks to the reign of idolatry and slavery !

Such consequences are the test of doctrines and enable us to refute them. I feel in the depth of my soul a burning anger, and I revolt against those doctrines which in order to attack God are obliged to bestow upon humanity, upon their time, upon all that is most honourable, most holy, and most beautiful, in humanity and in their age, the name of idolatry, the worst of names, the basest of all, because it expresses the most culpable of errors and the most shameful of slaveries.

In conclusion, the evolutionist doctrine desired to suppress God, and in order to this suppression availed itself of the methods of criticism; but criticism, on the contrary, has succeeded in ruining the evolutionist doctrine. Whether it be judged in itself or in its application to documents, to the facts of history and the Creed of the Church, this doctrine cannot be sustained; it must be repudiated by sound and free reason.

I know, moreover, that it is a weapon which begins to grow old-fashioned. Thanks be to God, I see the youth of our time arising, I hear the beating of their hearts, I recognise the conviction of their spirit; they are leaving you to rally to our side. The armour of criticism will soon be ancient armour to put in museums, whither we go to see how our ancestors fought. To-day we need other swords, other shields, other tactics.

Young men, shake yourselves free; set free your thought. You hunger and thirst for liberty. Now, reason is free when it has repudiated pantheism, atheism and criticism; it is free, when it keeps its vigorous principles, to accept what is good and reject what is evil.

Take in your hands the sword of charity. Those

who attack us are bold, scandalously bold when we consider their position. If it so happen that an honourable mind, given to wisdom and to charity, would place these at the service of its convictions and of its beliefs, they try to terrify him. In your turn, young men, sow the seed of terror in this worn-out world, because it knows only one thing —boldness in error; and because it has unlearnt the sublime and holy boldness of those who bear as symbol a crucifix in their hand. We will bring back to Jesus the crowds who die because they have Him not, and the desperate men who without Him seek vainly for the last word of life because they have lost the sense of eternity.

IV

THE CHIEF REASON FOR THE BELIEF IN THE DIVINITY OF JESUS CHRIST

AFTER having proved the vitality of belief in the Divinity of Jesus Christ, we turned our attention to the adversaries of this belief, asking them why they deny it. They answer: "We deny the Divinity of Jesus Christ because we deny God." The reason is a radical one. But an objection at once presents itself; if to deny were sufficient to destroy, a simple argument would overthrow the world. Those idealists who say, "The world does not exist," would at once with an argument— subtle indeed, but an argument all the same— have suppressed the world. Yet the world still rolls through all its shining spheres despite of the idealists. So, in spite of the denial of the Divinity of Jesus Christ, his Divinity remains.

We then said to those who deny that the Divinity of Jesus Christ is attested by public documents: What have you to say to the documents? They answer: We interpret them according to the rules of our exegesis so as to suppress the divinity which they contain. But it still remains in the facts of the history? Oh, we must pass the facts of history through the sieve of criticism, and criticism eliminates all those facts said to be divine.

But the dogmas which are the Creed of the great Catholic Church? These, say they, are the creation of human thought, and if the creation of human thought had any objective reality we should be under the full dominion of what is fantastic and absurd.

Such are, in sum, the answers of those who in our day suppress the Divinity of Jesus Christ. We have answered them in our turn: "The Atheism on which you base your contention is a doctrine which cannot bear the light of reason; your interpretation of the documents contradicts the fundamental law of interpretation; your historical criticism is in formal opposition to the law of evidence; your explanation of the genesis of Catholic dogmas, founded on a false psychology, only succeeds in making humanity incorrigibly idolatrous, whereof Jesus Christ would be the supreme idol."

After having studied the doctrine of those who deny, it is right that we should examine the faith of believers.

You believe in the Divinity of Jesus Christ! I

believe it too, with every fibre of my being—my whole life is staked on it. That proves nothing. I am but an atom; but the Catholic Church believes in it, and the Church is a third of the human race. Now, we ask if there is any foundation for our belief? We ask the faithful, we ask women why they believe, why they kiss the feet of Christ whom they call their God? I ask priests who hear me why they ascend the altar steps to offer a sacrifice, of which Jesus Christ is Himself the priceless Victim and eternal High Priest, for the priest is only the agent of this supreme Mediator. I ask the people, who still believe—peasants, workmen, children—why they say: "I believe in Jesus Christ, the only Son of God?" There are among believers some who do not know why they believe; and those who can say: "I believe for such and such a reason."

Do not disdain the first—as for me, I respect them as we respect children; for those simple people—women without culture; illiterate workmen, even though in these days they can read; men of science, who are skilled in the secrets of nature, yet accept the mysteries of God with the faith of a day-labourer; nuns who, though they live by the life of Christ, would perhaps find difficulty in defining their faith in Him—all those unconscious believers would answer: "I know not why I believe, any more than I know why or

how I breathe ; but what I see and feel is that if
there be in me any spark of good, any devotion,
and any virtue, if I can resist my passions and
master self, if I have any resignation in sorrow and
any firm hope, I owe these things to the faith in
Jesus Christ."

Popular reason.

This simple answer of the ignorant is far-reaching;
it is sufficient to confound the pride of unbelief. A
doctrine, indeed, is not proved only by the rational
basis on which we see that it rests, but it has an
equally secure justification in the sublime results
to which it leads and the virtues which it begets.

However, leaving out of question those believers
who cannot give a reason for their faith, I will
examine sincerely and loyally those who are under
the power of a deliberate belief. I will address
myself to the Church, great mistress of doctrine.
The Church has her reason for believing, and
I will ask her the motives for her unfailing
faith in the Divinity of Jesus Christ.

Church's reasons.

The arguments and motives for belief are so
numerous that to develop them at length would
need not one but twenty lectures, not one but
three or four volumes. These motives, as a whole,
can be brought under three categories.

We may appeal to all the ages which preceded
Jesus Christ and see them run their course ; above
all, among the people chosen of God to prophesy
and prepare for the Messiah ; and this is the

1° Prophecy

argument: "The Messiah announced from the beginning implied divinity; the Prophets called Him 'God with Man—Emmanuel.' Jesus Christ was Messiah; He was God."

2° Power & glory of Xⁿ. Church.

We may look at the times which have been since Jesus Christ, which the Catholic Church fills with the power of her declaration, with the splendour of her doctrine and her virtues, with the splendour of her deeds, and we may say: "The Church founded by Jesus Christ is a work which man could not originate or even maintain. The divinity of the work reveals the divinity of the workman; therefore He who was her founder was God."

3° the testimony of Xt. Himself.

And lastly, we may place ourselves at the centre of the history of Jesus Christ and say: "Jesus Christ declared Himself the Son of God, equal to the Father; therefore He was the Son of God, equal to the Father, and God as the Father." I pass over the first and second arguments, so as to

Consider the 3rd.

rest only on the third, for it resumes, dominates, and confirms the others.

2 questions.

The motive for belief founded on the testimony of Jesus Christ raises two questions: "Did Jesus,

1. Content of His testimony

the man whom history knows under that name, really declare Himself the Son of God, equal to His Father? and, if so, what is the evidential

2. Its value.

value of Him who uttered those words, the most extraordinary and momentous that human lips have ever pronounced?"

I will to-day only examine the former question, and establish the fact, absolutely incontrovertible from the historical point of view, that Jesus Christ declared Himself God. The fact has been denied; I affirm it. The fact has been disputed in the name of historical exegesis, in the name of this or that scientific criticism; I maintain it in the name of criticism, in the name of history, in the name of science.

[handwritten margin note: now Examine the 1st—the fact that He claimed to be God.]

And if I can get this conviction, which is the very soul of all my preaching, into your minds, I shall have gained a great victory. May the Spirit of Jesus Christ be with me and sustain me in this conflict, wherein the faith of His Divinity is at stake.

It is certainly true that Jesus of Nazareth, the carpenter, for that was His calling, did not leave the little town of Nazareth till He was twenty-nine or thirty years of age; He did not reveal himself until then, after a life of obscurity like our own. It is certainly true that this man, son of Joseph and of Mary, as He was called, whose fellow-countrymen and fellow-citizens pointed out His brothers and sisters, called Himself the Son of God, the only Son of the Father. It is quite certain that He proclaimed His equality with the Father?

Apart from this testimony I do not think that we can give the Divinity of Jesus Christ an indestructible basis. But if this testimony be established, I do not believe, as we shall see in a future lecture, that sound, impartial, independent reason—man's reason, not the reason of to-day or of yesterday, but of all time—can reject it. Reason must either rebel or submit, and you will therefore judge, when we examine the sum of our faith, how important it is to establish, in a positive, certain, invariable, unchanging manner, that Jesus Christ the Man, Jesus Christ the Son of Man, as He described Himself, did truly, without any possible ambiguity, according to history, declare Himself the Son of God.

No argument as to the reality of the claim formerly needed

In former times this declaration was readily ascertained; on opening the Gospels, to which was consigned the history of Jesus Christ, gathering together certain precise texts, sufficient to enlighten any unprejudiced mind, it was clear that both in His own circle, before learned men and before popular opinion, Jesus Christ openly and solemnly declared Himself the Son of God.

but it is now.

In our days an urgent need has arisen for surrounding this declaration with firmer guarantees, so as to raise it above all attack.

The scene at Philippi.

We all know the Gospel, there is not a believer here who cannot give a superficial proof of the assertion that Jesus Christ declared Himself the Son of God. The scene on the road to Cæsarea-

Philippi is easily brought to mind, so as to see the spot, the country-side, where Jesus Christ went His way; not, indeed, discouraged, but saddened by the faithlessness of that Galilean population who understood nothing of His spiritual Messiahship, and who would not listen to Him because they cared only for party politics. We see in spirit the spot where Jesus turned to His disciples and said: " Whom do men say that I am ? " " Some John the Baptist, and other some Elias, and others Jeremias, or one of the prophets : " for at that time it was believed that the spirit of the prophets revived after their death. And then Jesus said to Peter and to all His disciples : " Whom do you say that I am ? " and St. Peter, the spokesman of the little flock, answered : " Thou art Christ, the Son of the living God."

Evidently when he spoke thus Peter only gave words to the teaching which he had received from Jesus Himself; the result of the constant action of Jesus on His disciples persuaded them that He was so.

Criticism says that Peter, in professing that Jesus Christ was the Son of God, simply wished to declare that Jesus Christ was a man like any other, though somewhat superior. But there is one difficulty in this interpretation, which is that Jesus Christ said to Peter in solemn tone :

Interp. of Critics

of the Church .

" Blessed art thou, Peter, for having thus spoken. It is not flesh and blood "—that it is say, none of those aspirations which spring from the flesh and blood of poor humanity—" it is not flesh and blood which have revealed to thee who I am, but my Father who is in heaven"; and he added : " Therefore I will make of thee a foundation, on which I will build my Church, a rock against which the powers of hell shall not prevail."

No fair criticism can interpret the words of Peter otherwise than the Church has done, otherwise than as a recognition of the divine Sonship of Jesus Christ. Peter speaks, but Jesus Christ approves and confirms his words in a manner so extraordinary, so overpowering, that it is not possible to give to his expression any other than the grand and solemn sense which the Church has always recognised.

We may also quote texts which prove that Jesus Christ declared Himself the Son of God, but we meet at every turn a criticism which says : " Those words, ' Son of God,' must be understood either in the metaphorical or natural sense." No doubt they must. " Now, we cannot understand them as you do." But, I say, the Gospels are there and they teach us so. " The Gospels ! They were written at a later date."

These objections cannot move me, and I do not

multiply them, for the simple reason given in my
preceding lecture, that when we have to determine
the true sense of a book—not such a book as you
can get in the next street, at the fashionable shop
or library—when you have to give the sense of a
book which belongs to some one, which is the
property of an author or the patrimony of a
Church, you must examine this some one, this
author, this Church. Protestants may think me
severe, but I maintain that the Gospel belongs to
the Church alone, in whose womb it was conceived at the breath of the Spirit which lives
in her.

Such a book cannot be given over to the
interpretation of the first comer ; and if you ask
me whether Jesus Christ really declared Himself
the Son of God, I find in the books of the New
Testament those texts wherein this declaration
is contained, and I assert that the sole authentic
sense of those texts is given us by the Church,
which never ceases to proclaim it in the face of
the world.

This Church is here, and we are its members.
Not all, perhaps, who listen to me belong to her
organisation or her life, but the great majority
belong to her : the priests who hear me are her
representatives, and they are in touch with the
Body spread over the whole world, and with all
its members who cover the earth.

private interpn
not permissible

the Bible is the
Church's book.

This Church ceases not to say to you that Jesus Christ by His very word has affirmed His divine Sonship. She says it with an energy which has never failed, and, whether you wish it or not, you cannot disregard the constant declarations, which, beginning in the first century, have continued down to our day.

And that this is for a reason no one can gainsay, on which no other doctrine can depend, neither Buddhism, nor Mohammedanism, nor criticism, nor modern revolutionaries who seem to have a doctrine of revolution, nor modern revolutions.

The Church's witnessing function — continuous.

The reason is this : When Jesus Christ appeared He founded His Church ; that is to say, He gave His mandate to chosen men that they should repeat His word to all the ages, adapting it to all the ages. For eighteen hundred years the mandate of Jesus Christ has been carried out, starting from St. Peter, through all the Popes down to Leo XIII. What the Popes say is

The papal see

precisely that which Jesus Christ Himself said ; consequently, when they declare that Jesus Christ is the Son of God, they repeat the word which Peter was the first to receive from the mouth of Jesus, a word inexpressibly venerable and holy.

This has gone on without interruption ; if there has been an interruption, let historical and exegetic criticism tell me in what century and in what country ; and until it has done this I hold the declaration as authentic and continuous, and I maintain that the clearest light for the interpretation of the Gospel is the Church.

no evidence of break or lack of authenticity.

This attestation is perpetuated from age to age, down to our own days, and I declare it here in this very Church of the Madeleine. I am not declaring my individual thought : if I wished to express my individual thought I should do so elsewhere and not in this church. I come here to translate the thought of the Church, who has given me commission to do so. It is impossible for any one to maintain that the Church has lied at any given time, that she has betrayed the word of Jesus Christ which fell from His lips and has been transmitted from Pope to Pope, from priest to priest, from doctor, to doctor, until this blessed age of the nineteenth century, in which we hear the same great voice of the Church attesting the Divinity of her Founder—the Church always in action and always triumphant, because she has faith in this Divinity.

Preacher's testimony not personal but official. ✻

But I would give to the affirmation of Jesus Christ in regard to His own Divinity a force and a solidity which you would certainly wish to find in the fundamental truth which supports your faith. In the light of history I would show you that the declaration of His Divinity is not an

Xt's claim inextricably woven into the Gospel portrait.

✻ Formally, this logic is imperfect. The constituting of such a witness and the fact that it has been unvarying - say from 30 to 150 A.D. - and inerrant no proof to an unbeliever as much as the Divinity of Christ itself.

isolated phrase, nor even a solemn word spoken before the tribunal about to condemn Him to death, nor indeed a phrase which can be taken out of a life or a history without diminishing, mutilating, or falsifying the history or the life.

Take the Life of any great man—for example, the Life of Socrates—and you will find certain words which you can abstract from it, however sublime they may be, without detriment to the Life of Socrates, or of any other great man. But what is special and unique, and to this I call your attention, is that if you cut away the declaration of Jesus Christ affirming His own Divinity, you falsify and ruin the history of Jesus Christ. This declaration is part of the very body of His history, is so identified with it, so essential, that the disappearance or the alteration of the one implies and carries with it the alteration and the disappearance of the other.

J. Xt. willed to achieve a great work - a kingdom.

Whoever has studied the life of Jesus Christ, from whatever point of view he may have looked at it, must recognise that Jesus Christ willed to accomplish a work peculiar to Himself and planned by Him, that He founded and realised it in spite of a thousand obstacles, and in spite of all the forces allied against Him. To this work, as the documents unanimously demonstrate, Jesus Christ gave a name which in His thought distinguished it from every human work, a name

simple and profound, full of mystery and yet
clear, the name of the Kingdom of God. The
Kingdom of God expresses the whole work of
Jesus Christ, and you will perhaps allow my faith
to tell you how you should understand this
Kingdom. It is not possible to explain it badly
when one has lived a while with the Gospel which
contains its sublime and incomparable revelation.

The Kingdom of God is the supreme degree
of the universal evolution of things. Those who
take pleasure in great thoughts may well enter
into this kind of speculation.

This from the goal of evolution —

In the present day we only see reality under
the form of a collection of kingdoms—that is
the scientific word—the kingdom of matter, the
kingdom of life, the kingdom of animalism, the
kingdom of humanity ; and there atheistic science
stops. Jesus completes this majestic pyramid,
raising it to the infinite. At the hour when the
kingdom of humanity strove with the Empire of
Rome, and in which human civilisation, having
produced marvellous fruits, seemed worn out and
tending to its decline, under the weight of its
corruption, Jesus Christ said : "The kingdom of
heaven is at hand."

I seem to hear you object, that in your own
strength you have outrun old civilisations ; but that
is a mistake, and we, sons of the Crucified, who
have founded Christian civilisation, deny that the

modern progress due to it, even in those own it not.

kingdom of humanity as it now exists is natural progress, the necessary evolution of the anthropoid ape which you make the starting-point of modern humanity. No, we are not so simple as that. You are impregnated with the Spirit of Jesus Christ; it goes to your heart, and of that muscle He has the key; he holds your brain and has marked his name in its convolutions. You only exist by Christ; you may revolt against Him, but you cannot get away from Him. We call Him to your minds incessantly.

Now, here is the thought which dominates the whole work of Jesus Christ. Follow it, and you will see that, far from narrowing the horizon, faith extends it without measure.

Life works in and above matter. Now, life is nothing else than the participation in matter of a superior force, which I call vital force because we must give a name to it; and this participation constitutes a new kingdom, superior to that of brute and inorganic matter. And the kingdom of animal life is itself only the entrance into the kingdom of life of a superior force which we call sensation, and which is characterised by the passions and the faculty of recognising the individual. This new kingdom embraces the whole brute creation, and in regard to man I will give you a definition of the human kingdom which you will willingly accept, unbelievers though you be. The human kingdom is only the entrance of thought into animal life, of universal good and liberty into the will.

Man is indeed an animal, but an animal emerging from animalism in order to rule and conquer it. He does not entirely submit to the law of the brutes, he passes beyond their bounds ; and in passing beyond it he forms his own life, which is characterised by the perception of what is true, by the love of what is good and beautiful, and by the free mastery of his own actions.

Now, the subjection to animalism is not the same in all human beings. Thus I was reading recently in a scientific review an article on female criminals. The author, a learned Italian, maintains that there is much less crime in women than in men, and he gives this fundamental reason for his declaration : " Woman is less animal than man," and he declared that he was satisfied. For the honour of my sex I declare that I was not satisfied.

Such, then, is the human kingdom, and it is not final, for Jesus Christ came upon this earth to constitute a new kingdom, which He called the Kingdom of God. Now, just as life is nothing but the introduction of vital force into matter, just as the kingdom of animal life is the entrance of animal force into living beings, just as the kingdom of humanity is only the entrance of

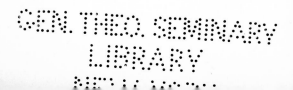

thought and liberty into the animal, so the kingdom of God is the introduction of the life of God and the Infinite into thinking and free humanity. This reign, which completes the universal evolution of things, is the work of Jesus Christ.

But since this participation in the life of God can be only realised by him who has God within him, and God as a good peculiar to himself, it results that this astonishing being, the greatest on earth, the most incomparable of all men—for no one except He ever had an idea of this superhuman work—Jesus Christ coming to found the kingdom of God in humanity must have had God in Him. Therefore He solemnly declared Himself to be the Son of God, equal to the Father, in full possession of the Spirit which He was to communicate to the faithful. Whence it follows that to set aside the declaration of Jesus Christ that He is the Son of God destroys at one blow his work and his history.

Jesus Christ was not only the founder of the divine work which I have just sketched, but also the moral lawgiver of humanity, promulgating His supreme and final law to those intelligent and free beings who would enter into his kingdom.

One of my great intellectual and religious satisfactions is that I see in the modern world, which often noisily boasts its incredulity, the

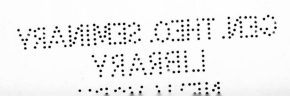

multitude drawn into the great furrow traced by
Jesus Christ. Most historians, and notably those
who call themselves critical, treat with unpardon-
able and even shocking lightness this essential
function of the Messiah. They rest on and are
pleased with the Sermon on the Mount. When
they have spoken of the birds poised in the air
while Jesus was speaking, when they have showed
us that verdant and flowery plain of Galilee
whereon He cast forth His word, when they have
emphasised the admirable poetry in which the
Master wrapped up His divine precepts, they
declare themselves satisfied. But they hardly
mark the superiority of Jesus to all other lawgivers; yet it only needs to examine the documents
to convince ourselves that, if others spoke as wise
men, Jesus alone spoke as God.

Some critics have even dared to deny the whole
originality of the Gospel scheme of morals, and
have set themselves to establish, against all evidence, that the grand Christian precepts are only
a new edition of Jewish and Pagan wisdom.

But there is plainly nothing falser than this.
First, an essential difference distinguishes the law
of Christ from all others. In fact, it cannot be
denied that it is the rigorous expression of absolute perfection, so that Jesus was able to say of
it: "Heaven and earth shall pass away, but my
words shall not pass away."

Now, see what other lawgivers have done. Moses, an inspired lawgiver, tolerated divorce. We know what were the ethics of Mahomet, conceding much to human weakness; it certainly cannot be denied that such concessions were clever, for he was only a man, and hence he could not impose on men absolute perfection ; he contented himself with putting evil under law and restraint. Since he was powerless to subdue the beast in human nature, he tried to muzzle it ; hence among other grave lapses in the Koran is the tolerance for polygamy, which the Christian conscience has always repudiated and stigmatised as shameful.

Jesus Christ was perfectly wise. He gave an absolute law without any diminution. He prescribed strict monogamy : one man, one woman.

While He said to his disciples : "Love your enemies," Mahomet said : "Death to the unbeliever." Mahomet, perhaps, thought himself very clever. Jesus Christ was not clever, He was absolute truth.

"But," you will say, "He is not obeyed." He is obeyed by his true disciples, and this because He has given not only precepts but power and spirit—the power of the Spirit of God—and He could not have given it if He had it not in Him.

While Moses has engraved the law on stone, Jesus Christ has engraved his law on the conscience ; to write in such a book one must be more than man. That alone is a new proof that the affirmation of His Divinity is a necessary condition for understanding Jesus Christ, even as a law-giver.

But He went further, and the deeper we pene-trate into this inherent function of His life we recognise that He transcends all other human beings and remains inexplicable without His Divinity. All the laws of the Gospel are summed up in this one word : We must believe absolutely in Jesus Christ. He has demanded nothing other than this from His disciples, from the people to whom He preached the Gospel as to all those to whom in all time He has transmitted his Law. To believe in Jesus as in God is the principle of all the laws of the Gospel and the great precept of Jesus.

"You believe in God," said the Master, "believe also in Me." It cannot be contested that the whole effort of His mission was to obtain faith in Him, unreserved faith. All His action was sub-ordinate to this primary virtue, which He demanded imperiously from all those who came to Him and sought to follow Him.

Now, I address myself to that elementary con-science which exists in all of us, and I say that no man can demand absolute faith from another man. I may believe in my friend or in my father, but I

do not believe in them with an absolute faith; I
believe in them only with a relative faith, a human
faith.   To believe in any one with absolute faith
is to give ourself over into his hands, is to have no
thought of our own, only the thought of him in
whom we believe; to have no longer any will of our
own, but to give ourself up to him without reserve.
If faith is complete, the abdication of will is also
complete.   If love is complete, we belong no more
to ourselves ; self is annihilated.

This is surprising to you! So it is to me.
You are offended at it! So am I.   What! give
oneself fully, unreservedly into the hands of
Christ!

I know our age and the passions which carry it
away ; individuality is the last principle which we
consent to sacrifice ; we desire to be ourselves, and,
jealous of our rights, we will not belong to any one.
Love which speaks so glibly of absolute, unlimited
confidence is deceived.   No one ever renounces
himself; he remains himself.

And in fact there is but one Being to whom we
can make this complete sacrifice, there is only
one Being who can demand it of us—God, because
He is absolute truth, absolute power, absolute
perfection.

Thus, when a free being, feeling that he has
only a relative truth, a weak will, a limited activity,
finds himself in presence of Him who demands a

total abdication of intellect before His word, of will before His moral law, of activity before His example, there are only two attitudes which can be taken : that of revolt or that of prostration ; that of revolt against Him who demands this total abdication, and, if it be a man, he is right ; or to prostrate himself because it is God who demands it of him—God, that is to say, absolute truth and perfection ; and this abdication becomes, then, the first and holiest of duties.

Now, that is just what Jesus Christ has demanded ; and in acting thus towards man He has represented Himself to man as God. O Master ! I bear witness to Thee before this congregation, witness from the very depths of my being, and I say : on the day when I saw that Thou didst demand the abdication of my thought before Thine, the abdication of my will before Thy law, the abdication of my activity before Thine example and Thy power, I made myself as nothing before Thee, remembering the words of Thy disciple : "I live, not now I : but Christ liveth in me."

In such a sacrifice there need be no regret. Those who renounce their own life find infinite, eternal life. I do not say that they realise it at once, but they find it in the hopes that swell the breast of believers and breathe into their heart those energies which none can know except they descend on him from above.

And I have only one wish to formulate, and that is, that all of you may hear the voice of Christ, and, recognising his Divinity, will not hesitate to become His disciples. Those who have given up all to Him have received a hundredfold, even in this world, in truth and peace; but those who know Him not are lost in a region of sadness and death, from which no human power can free them.

Answer, then, to the appeal of God to humanity, and may He make you new men this very day.

The affirmation of Jesus Christ, by which He declared His Divinity, is so identified and incorporated with His life that the life cannot be explained without it.

You are not ignorant of the Gospel history, and must needs recognise its dramatic character. I call every life a drama which in its evolution meets with terrible difficulties, which is oppressed by grave sorrows, whose end is a blood-stained tragedy. The life of Jesus Christ is, therefore, the most heroic drama, when we understand the psychological depths of the human being under whom the Divinity was concealed. It unfolded itself with headlong haste. After thirty years of a most tranquil existence, Jesus Christ revealed Himself, to enter on His public life, and in less than three years the drama came to an end—in a sudden, heroic, and terrible manner. Jesus

Christ evoked the most violent national and religious hatred, more violent than any other public man ever excited.

If we look at what passes in our present world when political passions are stirred and angry, we say, " Political passion is a frightful thing." But it is extremely superficial; I do not believe in political passion : strange as my words may seem, I do not believe in it, nor do the actors believe in it. It is more often a comedy than a tragedy. That which touches not the conscience is naught. Political hatred may produce a certain superficial agitation, and those who are not accustomed to it may call it tempestuous; but those who know what human nature really is are not troubled, and let the storm go by. But religious hatred is terrible. It is the only one which comes from the depths of the soul and goes to its depths. Now, Jesus Christ was above all others persecuted by the hate of hates—religious hate ; and, in order to account for that drama in which his life ended, we must seek the cause of this hatred, the motive wherefore He was so violently rejected by the people to whom He addressed Himself.

If you read the history of Jesus Christ according to unbelieving criticism, you will see in it that He desired to found a new religion. That is a mistake; He never spoke of such a thing.

The truth is, that Jesus Christ deeply wounded the self-love of His countrymen; unmasking the hypocrisy of the Pharisees and doctors of the law, who violated its essential commands. In holy anger, He armed Himself with the scourge to smite and confound them when He saw them make the house of his Father a den of thieves. Thus He raised against Himself all the interests and passions which could so easily cover themselves with a mask of religious hypocrisy.

But if you penetrate the depths of Jesus Christ's life-drama, you will be convinced that this hatred was provoked against Him because He affirmed, with a truth always increasing and always more overwhelming, that He was the Son of God, equal to His Father.

You will, perhaps, ask why such a declaration shocked, revolted, offended the Jews? It was that their principal dogma—the dogma of the unity of God—was for them, and especially at that time, the object of a superstitious veneration. Their monotheism went so far as to deny the divine Trinity, although many transparent allusions were made to it by their prophets.

We can with difficulty form an idea of the intolerance and fanaticism of those people in relation to Jehovah—the only God, the Rock, the Foundation, as they called Him. Therefore the fury of the Scribes, the doctors, and the people reached a sort of paroxysm when they heard Jesus proclaim His Messiahship and His divine Sonship, declaring that He had received all from God His Father, and that He was equal to Him.

Such a doctrine exasperated the Jews. They could not contain their indignation against Him who appeared to them the greatest of blasphemers; they took up stones to stone Jesus Christ.

How great an example is He for all those who, bringing truth before the world, have suffered for her sake! How often, in studying the life of the Master, I have fallen on my knees at the sight of the indomitable courage with which He went to His death! Certainly, He knew well that in giving Himself out as the Messiah, Son of God, equal to the Father, He would excite the fury of religious authority in the people among whom He declared his doctrine. He knew well that the Jews, the doctors, the learned, the Pharisees, would be offended, and give vent to all their rage; that the High Priest would condemn Him as a blasphemer, and send Him to death. He knew this, and He went directly and boldly to Calvary. Religious hatred, excited to paroxysm, did not shrink from judicial murder to punish Him who made Himself equal to God.

Such is the true reason for which Jesus was

condemned to death ; this must be declared openly
in the face of those who deny the Divinity of
Jesus Christ.   As they are obliged by this denial
to mutilate His teaching, they must misrepresent
the truth of the drama which terminated His
great life.   But the testimony is indestructible and
invincible.   Not only did Jesus declare Himself
in formal terms the Son of the living God, but
He also with prophetic solemnity declared Himself
to possess the inexpressible attributes of God.

"Hereafter," He said to the High Priest "you
shall see the Son of Man sitting on the right hand
of the power of God, and coming in the clouds
of heaven."

No criticism can ever prevail against the
evidence, the solemnity and boldness of such
declarations.   It cannot deny them without giving
the lie to history ; and if it accept, it cannot
understand them.   They have indeed no meaning
except for those believers who recognise in Jesus
Christ not merely a man, but the only Son of
God, Him who was at the beginning of things
and will appear at the end of the world and of all
things to set them in order and to judge.

Let not the unbelievers smile.   I know you
well, as I know myself ; for we all of us have in
us a leaven of incredulity.   You ask, What is the
end of all things and when will it come ?   You
who think that you have probed everything, do

not look so far and therefore refuse to understand it. The end of all things has not need of your understanding, it will manifest itself to you with the rapidity of lightning. Our sun will expire as other suns have expired. There will come a moment when all will end for us, the moment when the Master of heaven and earth, the Judge of all men, Jesus of Nazareth, will appear in His glory and His triumph. May you be able to stand before Him!

O Christ! Who hast declared Thyself so plainly to be the Son of God; Thou Who hast entered so far into this humanity which Thou bearest by the virtue of Thy word, be Thou with us! I know that men disfigure Thee, but the records which set forth thine image, the Church which guards Thy worship, the believers who bear Thee living within them, have the power of maintaining Thee in the midst of this world, carried away by all terrors, fooled by all kinds of aberrations, which knows not where it is going. But Thou knowest whither we go. Thanks be to Thee, our life is filled with divine hopes; we would live by Thee—that is to say, by God Himself, having done good after Thine example, having loved Thee, having adored Thee in Thy wisdom, Thy goodness, Thy power and Thy Divinity.

H

V

THE WORTH OF THE TESTIMONY OF JESUS AFFIRMING HIS DIVINITY

WE have established it as an historical, undeniable, indestructible fact that Jesus declared His Divinity or His divine Sonship in an absolute equality with His Father, as He expressed Himself. We have shown that this declaration was not a simple phrase isolated from His teaching or from His life, but that it made part of the body of His work and teaching, and that it was the centre of the whole drama of His heroic and divine existence.

We must, as I have already promised, examine this declaration and criticise it rationally.

I trust that no believers here will be surprised at the word rational criticism applied to the sayings of Jesus. Faith is not a blind and impassive action of reason; every thinking man has a full right to examine the motives for belief before he believes, and he ought only to bend the knee when he recognises the wisdom of these motives.

Thus, when Jesus publicly declared His Divinity, do not suppose that humanity crouches like an obedient slave : humanity has in itself men who reason, men who think, who know, and those men have examined and criticised the testimony of Jesus. This examination and this criticism are constantly renewed ; we will put them into practice to-day, and we will ask in our turn what is the evidential value of the declaration of Jesus which declares His Divinity and His divine Sonship.

Jesus is a witness. He speaks and declares that He is the Son of God, equal to the Father. What is the worth of this declaration before free, enlightened, and impartial reason ? If it has any worth, reason must recognise it ; if it has not, the duty of reason is to repudiate it.

You will notice that the unheard-of and prodigious saying by which Jesus declared His Divinity has commanded the attention of humanity and of human conscience in spite of all sorts of objections. In spite of the religious reason of the Jews; in spite of the cultivated reason of the Pagans, many of whom still exist ; in spite of the subtle and shifting reason of those who are called heretics and are unable to accept frankly the yoke of faith, in spite of all this, in spite of the hostility of some and the indifference of others, it has impressed the conscience of humanity. This is a surprising fact when we think of the many sublime words which have fallen from the lips of human genius, and left no trace or have remained as the possession of only a few, while those of Jesus have triumphed over human pride and implanted themselves like a barb in the quick of human conscience.

I who speak to you have received this barb deep in my heart; I am here among you to interpret this saying, to defend it in the midst of a world that disdains it, not only by the lips of the common people but by the lips of the masters of public opinion. After half a century of life, and not having been by any means brought up in the midst of the desert or in the sheepfold, but at the feet of the doctors of our time, I am here to speak to you of the declaration of Jesus and to prove that it has its value.

It is strange and surprising, even to me, how, after eighteen hundred years it has lost nothing of its persuasive force. It is true that on reflection it is nearer to us than it seems at first. In fact if we consider what separates us from that moment in which Jesus on the road to Cæsarea, and before the Jewish authorities, declared his divine Sonship, and announced his return in the clouds to judge the living and the dead, we find we are separated from that time by two hundred and sixty three Popes succeeding each other uninterruptedly in the government of the Church, with an average reign of seven to eight years— that is to say, twenty generations. Now two men to each generation for nineteen hundred years is about forty men only.

In truth we can almost say that we touch and hear Jesus Christ. Forty men are not enough to stifle the powerful voice which has cried aloud this truth, more powerful still, and of which it has been the mission of the Popes to repeat again and again the immortal echo. I repeat this assertion once more, for it has entered into the very depths of my conscience, and I justify it before you after having in the first place established its rigorous authenticity.

The critical examination of testimony raises two questions : the first relative to the tenor of the testimony, the other relative to the worth of the witness.

If we establish the tenor of the testimony from the point of view of reason and if, from the same point of view, we establish the evidential value of Him who affirms, the duty of every impartial spirit, freed from prejudice, is to receive the testimony and bow to the authority of the witness. I hope that I may show you that the affirmation by which Jesus declared His Divinity is of reasonable worth, and that He is a witness whose authority bears sway over consciences.

The tenor of a testimony must precede all examination, for that which a witness says to us may
be absurd, contradictory, and inconceivable, and
then we have a right to set it on one side by
opposing to it the previous question. When,
therefore, Jesus declared His divine Sonship, we
ask what was, and what is now, the tenor of such
a declaration.

Evidently when we go to the root of such a
saying we find there the essential idea of the
union of the divine with the human nature in
one and the same person which is divine—I need
not examine this point—that is to say, Jesus.
Therefore the declaration of Jesus implies the
union of the divine and human natures in His
person ; two natures in one person is the tenor of
the message.

You must not confound, and you must not seek to
get to the bottom of that which has no bottom and
which surpasses all your comprehension, because,
whenever man touches the divine, he comes upon a
being who is above his grasp and comprehension ;
he can recognise the reality and see it superficially,
but he cannot penetrate its depth. In hearing the
declaration of Jesus in the sense which it implies, we
must be content to examine whether it presents to
human reason anything contradictory or absurd.

I know that there are atheistic doctrines which
declare without discussion : " From the moment

you speak of God as a personal being we cannot listen to you, for there is no God." Pardon me, atheistic doctrines are not human reason : they are individual reason narrowed by a system which is not only doubtful but false, which reason shatters when it gives free play to its essential qualities. And when I speak of examining the declaration of Christ, it is certainly not that I may bring it before the tribunal of restricted and systematised reason, but of essential, eternal, popular reason.

The union of the human and divine natures need not imply anything contradictory or absurd. If there were, as certain heretics have asserted, any confusion of nature, we should have a right to revolt against it, but there is no confusion here ; we speak only of a union without confusion, without mixture—an union of two natures in one Person who is at the same time God and Man. It is in this quality that Jesus is adored by Christians.

Now, not only is there nothing in this contradictory and absurd; but if, going further, we consider the nature of man, the nature of God, and the general laws of the universe in which such union is brought about, we shall see an admirable convenience and harmony between the declarations of Jesus and our reason.

I look first at man, investigate his nature and inquire into his aspirations. I ask what is the

desire of man. Man in the depths of his nature
is irresistibly moving towards the Infinite, as I
have already said in this pulpit.   Man never
stops; the truth he contemplates is limited,
the love which enkindles him is limited, the
perfection he attains is limited.   But he ever
seeks for more perfection, more love, and more
truth.   Man is ever pressing against the limits
which confine him. This is his character and
his privilege. He is constantly going forward,
insatiable, panting and athirst.   This is his glory,
and by this he is the ever-growing king of
creation.

As he is ever going forward his goal must
be the Infinite. This aspiration dominates and
contains all others, it is concealed in them;
nothing created can satisfy the desires of man,
while all that brings God near to our nature
moves its depths, and raises it above itself.

Nor should we be astonished that the declaration of Jesus, revealing in His person the highest
union of the divine and human natures, finds an
echo in man's conscience.   On that day man felt
that he could see, hear, and attain to God, and
that his deepest aspiration was satisfied.

The union of the human and divine natures is
no less deeply in harmony with God than with man.
For so far as we know God, and in truth we know
Him very little, we know of His inner life only

what He is pleased to tell us. Now He is called
by a name which reveals His nature better than
all the systems of philosophy, whereof the brightness pales in contrast with that glory which has
its source in His very name. Pagans called God
the Best, the Perfect, *Optimus*; Christians, better
taught by Jesus, gave Him the name which has
more life in it, a name more sublime and deeper,
but which has the same sense. They called Him
the Father—*Pater*. I do not know that there are
any two other names given to God which are
worth the trouble of recalling : and when we seek
the idea which is hidden under these two ex-
pressions we find that of goodness.

There is, indeed, no higher name than that of
Father. Some who hear me may say Mother;
but the mother is a part of the father, and in order
that the mother may be perfect she must make
herself one with the father, who, unless he render
himself unworthy, remains the supreme lord of the
household. The father, then, the ultimate source
of being, is goodness. Now all that is good seeks
to communicate itself.

Whence it follows that the supreme law of God,
if indeed we can speak of law in relation to
Him, is a law of outpouring, of communication.
Whence it follows again that every idea which
implies the communication of God with His
creature is conformed to the nature of God

Himself, the best of beings, the father above all.

Now the Divinity of Jesus Christ supposes the most perfect gift of God to the human being, and by Him to all humanity. It is not strange, then, that such a revelation finds immediate access to the human conscience, which is always stirred by goodness.

For we see that the universe which science studies, investigates and seeks to rule, the universe in which is brought about the union of the human and divine natures, unfolds itself, according to an admirable plan, in the unity of a growing, powerful, and irresistible synthesis.

Now, if we examine with the eye of science the law which rules these vast evolutions, we shall admit that the great phenomena produced within this immense reality into which we are cast as imperceptible atoms is always and everywhere an increasing union. All inferior forces tend to rise towards the superior force and unite themselves to them, obeying a mysterious and irresistible attraction. If we look at matter, it always strives to increase; but in order that it should increase, it must unite itself to another power having dominion over it, which is called life. When beings are living, then, in order that they may gain greater fullness of life they must unite themselves to a superior principle transcending matter, which is called animal sensation, and which by means of instinct constitutes the animal kingdom. That the animal kingdom should increase in its own life it must unite itself to a superior principle not in itself, which is called intellect and liberty. It, then, becomes man who unites thus in himself, in the unity of his personality, many kinds of nature : matter first, of which he is formed ; life, because he has all that characterises the vegetable kingdom ; next, sensation, as having all the powers of an animal. But this animalism and sensation, this life and matter, are governed by a superior principle which is called intellect and liberty, and by this man becomes the synthesis of things, the king of the universe and of the creation, and of which he contains all the elements in sum.

And there the unbeliever and the atheist stop ; man is for them the final word of the cosmos ; I will go further, and man will go further. I will follow him, I declare that I will be with him, so as not to betray that nature whose aspirations will never stop here below, which, incessantly projected outside itself, seems drawn to a transcendent, intangible reality ; that is to say, towards the Infinite, towards God. Only—and here I find myself in agreement with them—man may go on for ever without attaining an end, because man is finite. But if so, it is strange that the finite does not satisfy him ; the finite after a time leaves him

tired and out of heart. When man has resolved
one problem, he wishes to solve another; he seeks
a new solution, deeper and greater. When he has
found one force, he is not satisfied, and does not
rest content with it; he wishes for another force;
he starts again, he goes forward from victory to
victory.

We look at the children of science who fear to
stand still, and find them a superb army. We see
them in their laboratories, ever restless, wishing
to master new forces. The children of light may
seek these unknown powers, may tend towards the
infinite which they will never attain; across all
reality the world will extend around them, and
they will never exhaust it. They will see star
after star, nebulæ after nebulæ, and when they
can handle explosive forces like harmless sand
they will only know the first word of all these
forces, because other forces more irrepressible are
yet to be discovered, not in order to terrorise us,
but to overthrow the obstacles which matter op-
poses to our triumphant march.

Men will seek and find the secrets of disease,
discover microbes and know that these will give
birth to others; they will open the doors of the
world of the infinitely little, which will astonish
them by its smallness and defy them by its
power. Men will study all systems, and when they
have found means of harmonising them, humanity

will take new and unforeseen departures; the unexpected will upset all social science like a flash of lightning.

The search will continue; we shall seek to place our fingers on the living point, the central point, the only point which is the key of all.

Yet this point will remain beyond the grasp of the scientific man and the philosopher. It is like that number which is the key to the power of things; we cannot attain it, we shall never attain it, unless it reveal itself to us. It is the only solution of the human problem.

Man, such as we know and see him, insatiable in intellect, activity and will, is very terrible in his power; we fear him and despair of him. St. Paul has said with energetic eloquence: "If in this life only we have hope in Christ, we are of all men most miserable!"

There is nothing more awful than a traveller on his route who never comes to the end of it; nothing more lamentable than breathless activity in search of an ever-receding goal; nothing more horrible than the fate of a man who, hungry and thirsty, desires to moisten his lips at a living fountain, and always finds himself confronted by a new disillusion.

Thus I understand those who are in despair and revolt, those who faint by the way, those who blaspheme, having no revelation of God; I pity them and would fain raise them and stanch their wounds. I know that man must despair who can find no solace for his heart and no cheer for his thoughts. I pity him with all the depths of my soul. I have a horror of those who are satisfied and full; those who are satisfied are false gods. They have made idols of their wretched selves and lack nothing; they have the vanities, the goods, the joys of this world; they have feasting, pleasure, luxury, and power; they possess all and grow fat. They are the fortunate, and are insolent in their good fortune.

Christ, in his gentle and divine language, said: "Blessed are the poor, blessed are they that hunger and thirst after justice, blessed are they that weep, because they have not what they would in this world." O God, I say the same as Thou, now that Thou hast transformed my human wrath into Thy infinite gentleness. Blessed are they because God has done what man could not do: the Incarnation is the coming of God among men—that is to say, the union of the divine and the human natures.

That is the solution of the problem; henceforward man need run no more without hope of gaining his end. He need no longer hope without satisfaction for his hope, he need no longer be restless and panting, for what he would he has: God is with him and in him, He is amongst us, and being amongst us He but completes the great movement of the universe into which we are flung. Man has already united all the elements in the unity of his person and of his nature ; he wanted one thing alone to complete the drama of the universe, he wanted God. It was necessary that all created forces should be joined to Him and that a divine Person should unite in an indivisible, indestructible unity all that exists—matter, soul and spirit.

So the flesh is exalted ; the mere animalism of brutes with its gross instincts is raised to the order of divine things. And poor liberty, tottering reason, the frail power of a day, are raised to the will, the wisdom, and the power of the Infinite. Philosophers who seek the universal synthesis can find none greater, nor an ideal more beautiful and more adorable. The young who dream noble dreams can imagine none equal to that which is contained in the declaration of God made man. O Son of Heaven and Earth, all that thou hast willed in thy boldest and fullest aspirations thou now holdest in the faith and the infinity of thy hope.

After having examined the tenor of the declaration by which Jesus attests His Divinity, we have to examine the evidential worth of Jesus Himself.

When we have to appreciate any witness—above

all, one whose deposition has reference to points of sovereign importance, we have first to examine his honesty, then his worth or intellectual competence, and lastly, to examine his life, to know whether the actions of this witness correspond to his words.

No one can complain of these demands, which are only just. The witness finds himself in one of the highest situations which man can fill, he demands one of the most difficult things to obtain: by the simple fact that he makes a statement, he asks our faith, and we have the right to demand that he be worthy of it. Man is distrustful, and he has reason to be so, for he cannot blind himself to the perversity and falsehood common among men.

This being so, as soon as a witness presents himself we have a right to ask him who he is and examine his moral honesty, as the first guarantee of the truth of his testimony.

Popular good sense—always very keen, and for which I have more consideration than I have for certain philosophers—popular good sense is never deceived. It has inspired human justice to demand an oath from the witness. Naturally, Atheism hates an oath, and I will track Atheism into this last refuge.

Popular feeling demands an oath, for the simple reason that an oath declares the presence of the

God invoked. A man who takes an oath raises himself to a great moral height, unless he is perjured. He steeps himself in, identifies himself with, that God whom he invokes; and as God is the chief good, as God is the eye that surveys all things, as God is the Judge from whom there is no appeal, as God is the perfect Being, the man who takes an oath partakes, by that very fact, in the nature of Him who is good, who is perfect, Him who knows all and sees all; and he is at that moment sacred, even though in his ordinary life he were the lowest of men.

The atheist will tell me that my God is but an idol; that his own conscience is enough for him. His conscience! I am glad to hear it. But what is conscience to a man who believes in nothing? The atheist will say it is the voice which tells him to do good. But who is the judge? Who, in the last appeal, will pronounce that you have done well? And if conscience tells you that you may kill, that you may burn—for there are consciences which say so—then you will say: "In the name of my conscience I have killed and I have burned, because I ought to do so."

That, you will answer, is an aberration, a madness, which the social order rejects. But there is no social order except the eternal

I

justice of God, unless it be the reign of the strongest. The weakest must yield to force; the strongest will always be right.

Thus, either conscience is reduced to itself, as atheism will have it, in which case it falls as a baseless edifice, and may justify crime; or conscience is the reflection of absolute, eternal, immutable justice, which punishes and rewards, in which case it is the force which sustains all things, and we may venerate, protect, and develop it.

Oh, Mother! shelter the conscience of thy children, nourish them with the milk of justice as with thine own! Oh, Master! when children are placed in thy hands, take care that conscience enters into the very depths of their being! Oh, Priest! make conscience penetrate yet deeper—even to those depths which Christ has touched! Oh, Legislators! remember conscience! when you declare a law, you say that you maintain social order; but know that conscience alone maintains law, and that God alone maintains conscience. Think of the generations to come who, perhaps, will be victims of that blind atheism of which self-interest is the sole and worthless guide.

Thus every witness must have the honesty of conscience as guarantee of his word. It is necessary and right that he take an oath, to invoke the eternal justice which is above him. Thenceforward we have faith in him, because being near to God he has a hold on eternal morality, eternal justice, and eternal perfection.

Again we ask, what is the worth of Jesus from the standpoint of moral sanctity ? Would that I could repeat to you here, as my sole demonstration, the history of that life of our Master—that life of the Man who said He was the Son of Man while He declared Himself the Son of God ! No fairer beauty has ever shone on the surface of the earth—never has a like dignity, a like sanctity, honoured and dazzled the human race. I except no name in history : you may scrutinise all its pages, and will find no one single example of a man who has attained such a height as He.

You, who know what man is, are aware that the ideal of virtue is always above and beyond us ; that we shall never attain it : a very little sincerity reveals to us our failures, our moral poverty ; no one can say that he is perfect and without reproach. We may here and there find people who boast themselves of some virtue or other ; well-balanced minds, who moderate their instincts ; generous hearts which are open to kindness and mercy ; pacific natures, who seek to promote peace and harmony. But there is a

vast difference between these partial virtues and
the entire perfection and saintliness which shines
in Jesus.

Man is drawn in three directions: by his
conscience, his interests, and his instincts. Conscience leads him to goodness and honourable
dealing; interest attracts him to what is useful;
instincts stimulate him to pleasure. Now conscience is frail; it often hesitates in finding its
way, and is powerless always to comprehend
and realise perfect good; the eager pursuit of
interest imprisons us in selfishness; pleasure
excites our appetites and leads to a thousand
excesses.

In Jesus was nothing of the sort. He escaped
the fatality of corruption, His conscience was the
manifestation of the will of His heavenly Father;
He always felt this will in Him, He said it and
repeated it. He made this will the law of all
His acts; His entire life was at the service of the
divine will; He even said that His meat was to
do the will of His Father in heaven. You will
notice that in the Gospel there is never any
question of the conscience of Jesus, but that He
spoke always of the will of His Father. Now
the will of God being perfection, Jesus, in
following this obediently, realised absolute perfection in His human existence.

He had but two interests: the business of His

Father; when only twelve years old we see in a remarkable passage of the Gospel that the business of His Father was His constant preoccupation; the glory of God, as we should say now. Secondly, the higher interests of man, the glory of God, for Jesus, was in reality that God should reign among men. He desired that instead of blind instinct, and deceitful ambition, whether personal, patriotic, or humanitarian, the will of God should be in them as it was in Him, thus raising their domestic, patriotic, and humanitarian interests to the height of the Infinite.

That was the human interest which Jesus sought. All His life, from the moment that He entered on the scene to His last hour, was consecrated to the triumph of His Father and to the good of man.

The course of His daily life was admirable. If you will study the course of your own, you will see how sordid it is, but study the daily life of Jesus during the two years and a few months comprised in His public career; it was entirely divided between the good of His Father and the good of man.

He rose early, before the sun, and began the day by prayer; He went apart from human habitation into the solitary fields; for prayer is difficult in the tumult of human affairs. Then, when He had prayed, His disciples who sought Him came to Him. He said then : " Let us go and preach to the multitudes and take to them the word of life." He often said to His apostles, " Children, let us go and preach."

Having entered into the villages they came to Him, they brought Him by hundreds, multitudes of sick, lame, blind, paralysed, those struck by fever or epilepsy, and madmen. The crowd was so great that He had not time to eat, and it was difficult for Him to make His way among them. Men came to be healed and He healed them, there was a chorus of blessings from all those who regained their health. His life was one stream of good actions ; He pardoned those who demanded a higher life, and even argued in order to get His doctrine into rebellious intellects, seeking only the good and the glory of His Father.

There is no mention of pleasure in the life of Jesus. His only joy consisted in doing good. When He had been able to heal, to bring back men to faith and to transform their natures, He felt an unspeakable joy through His whole being.

One fact has always struck me in His life ; in the midst of the fatigues of His apostleship, He forgot to eat. " Eat, Master, eat ! " His disciples said to Him ; and Jesus answered them " My meat is to do the will of Him that sent me."

Such is a rapid sketch of the moral integrity of Jesus, I would say of His heroic sanctity ; for if you measure the sanctity of a man by the perfection of the rule he obeys, no sanctity can be comparable to that of Jesus who had no other will than that of God, whose life never derogated from that sublime law ; of Jesus, who knew only the eternal interests of man which are identical with the glory of his Father ; who, moreover, tasted no joys but the immaterial joys of the spirit.

There is, for us, no proof of our own uprightness apart from the solemn fact of a true oath. There is no certain, evident, and infallible sign to enable us to recognise the righteous man.

The righteous man is he who strikes his breast and is humble of heart, the penitent sinner who mourns and weeps. When you see a man who has no repentance, only two hypotheses are possible : either God has raised him and assumed him into His divine perfection, or he is not sincere.

Jesus never repented. When He died upon the cross, He asked pardon for His executioners ; history does not record one single word dealing with the confession of His own moral sorrows, for He knew none.

The witnesses who narrated His life as it unfolded itself before their eyes have given testimony to a sanctity which has no equal in the world and is unstained by any weakness.

Those who have not sinned may stand erect, but those who have sinned must bow before Him who was always the well-beloved Son of the Father, before Him in whom His enemies themselves could never discover in the name of justice the smallest blot, the smallest imperfection.

He is there in the rays of His glory, in His charity and sanctity; and, whatever was the abuse which assailed Him, no word has ever tarnished the moral beauty of His life. He never knew human frailty.

He remains alone upright in the midst of prostrate and repentant beings, as the ideal of justice, of moral beauty, and consequently of sincerity. When He speaks, to declare a fact or a truth, however transcendent the fact, however mysterious the truth, He must be heard; He is the first of witnesses, the witness above all others, the witness to whom faith cannot be refused.

A witness, moreover, must be competent in the matter about which he testifies. Now is Jesus a competent witness to His own divinity? I am not speaking, for it is useless, of His intellectual worth in the precise sense of the word; nor will I speak of the sublimity of His reason and of His mind, in regard to those eternal truths which He

enounced and the absolutely lofty morality which
He promulgated, or of the doctrinal teaching
which fell from his divine lips.

I will rather confine myself to making you
understand his competence, as a witness to his
divinity.

You will notice that the divinity of Jesus
declared by Him, is a fact of consciousness, an
inner fact, a fact of which He had not only the
feeling, but the vision ; a fact which we can no
more grasp than we can grasp, for example, the
respect or the affection of whose existence you
assure me.

You say to me : "I esteem you." I do not see
it, but your conduct demonstrates it to me, and I
believe this interior and invisible fact.

Jesus said : "I am the Son of God." To
the High Priest who asked Him solemnly, He
answered : "Thou hast said it, and hereafter thou
shalt see the Son of Man coming in the clouds
and sitting at the right hand of the Father."
Note this well ; here is no theory. Jesus never
made a theory or a system like human moralists
or philosophers. It is a fact, a divine and transcendent fact, which we cannot grasp, but to which
He bears witness. His word is an attestation for
which He demands faith. Now when we have
the attestation of a fact of consciousness, there are
only two hypotheses : either the witness is mis-

taken about himself and about the fact of consciousness which he attests, or he does not deceive himself. If he deceives himself, he is under an hallucination; if he does not deceive himself, he is a wise man.

The dilemma is absolute. Jesus declared that He was the Son of God. In saying this, was He wise or was He under an hallucination? To put the question is to solve it. Those who know the life of Jesus will never admit the hypothesis of hallucination; and I would say to those who have not read his life: When a man under an hallucination speaks, he can but disturb for a brief moment the little world in which he lives. Those under an hallucination can sometimes make people talk about them in a town, it may be a Greek town in which men love what is new, and there are Greek towns in all centuries; they may at most bring upon them, together with the attention of the light and frivolous populace, the attention of a few men of science; but the world passes on, and they are but as a little pebble which an engine crushes as it goes.

But when the declaration of a man has roused a whole people, as did the affirmation of Jesus, excited to revolt the religious authorities, the Sadducees, all the great families of Israel who took part in the government of their country; when it has had the power to revolutionise a whole nation; when it has found the way to enter into the Roman world, and burst it all in sunder, like an explosive, yet not to terrify but to renew this rotten people, those old Romans, those sceptical philosophers, those proud senators, those free livers, those gamesters, those epicureans, that whole multitude crushed under vice, sensuality and indifference; when this declaration has entered there, stirring the whole of this corrupt humanity; when not content with exploding the civilised world, it penetrated also into those barbarous nations which hurled their forces against the crumbling walls of Imperial Rome, and subdued their consciences; when at this very day, in this world weary of doctrines and philosophy, weary of writers and politics, and seeking something else to move it; when at this day, in this world, this declaration succeeds in keeping everything vibrating with emotion, I call on you to say these are not words and declarations of a man under an hallucination.

You see this as well as I do. When such a word penetrates in this manner everywhere, making its way through the mind and conscience of man, overthrowing peoples and civilisations, we must be sincere and bow before its power, for it is no longer man, but God who passes by.

The words of Jesus declaring his divinity come

before us clothed with a character which I must needs specify, for it adds a supreme guarantee to their power. See with how divine an art the Son of God deigned to treat humanity. He would not utter this word as a philosopher, or as a great thinker, or as a politician might have done; He willed that this word, which suffers no hesitation nor doubt, should be sealed by his blood and his death.

For it is a fact of history that Jesus suffered and died for declaring that He was the Son of God, and in acting thus He has clothed his declaration with a persuasive power which no human word can claim.

Indeed, I know only two sorts of words, those which bring us praise, which lead us to glory and make us live; or those which compromise us, raise up public opinion against us, and lead us to persecution and death.

When I see my contemporaries live by their words, gain the glory of them, the glory of public opinion, of their rivals and of their age—if those words are beautiful I accept them willingly; but the triumphant happiness of these men makes me pause, and if it is a matter of testimony I hesitate before I believe them. I say to myself: those men are so fortunate, perhaps it is their personal interest and not truth which inspires them.

You cannot but have that thought, and yet to have it is not to be cynical.

But if, on the contrary, a man utters a word, formulates a doctrine, which must encounter the opposition and the hatred of his people, even threats, persecution and death, we cannot but esteem that man. To suffer and to die for the truth, to be treated because of it as a public male-factor, is the noblest fate and the privilege of prophets. Welcome, then, suffering and death, let them escort us who bring to humanity the word and the truth of God.

Accompanied by suffering and seeing death before us, we pass through men and force an in-different or hostile multitude to bow before us, when we are no more, and to recognise the truth to which we have testified.

Jesus was the first to walk in this heroic and glorious path, misunderstood by his people and by almost all his contemporaries, Jews, Romans and Greeks, listened to by only a few ignorant men. He went to death as a victim who knew whereto He was destined, saying: "I, when I am lifted up, will draw all men to me." And, indeed, He whom the Jews crucified after having rendered this bloody and final testimony to the truth which He declared, has drawn men to Him by a movement which the ages have not retarded.

There is, then, in this world a greatness which

can resist everything, that of a truth-telling witness. It is by this witness that families live. It is by a testimony from Him that woman believes in the fidelity of her husband, that a husband believes in the fidelity of his wife. By this witness justice exists, by this witness that kingdoms endure, by this witness the Church lives. By this testimony the divinity of Jesus Christ is implanted in the human conscience.

And yet, among all these witnesses, He who by his competence is the most indisputable, He who can claim by his death the most absolute confidence in the divinest word which was ever registered in the annals of martyrs, is Jesus Himself.

O, Jesus, Witness, whose humble disciple I am, Thou truly standest in the divinity of Thy testimony. The world may pass away and hurl reproaches at Thee after the fashion of Thine own people who did not fear to call Thee "Samaritan, and possessed of the devil," that terrible word of insult and of blasphemy. Yes, the world may pass away, but Thou remainest in the rays of Thy martyr's glory, in Thy sanctity ; and we come to kneel before Thee, saying in the words of the centurion : " Truly, this man is the Son of God."

VI

THE DIFFICULTIES OF THE ACT OF FAITH IN THE DIVINITY OF JESUS

AFTER having established as an historical and undeniable fact, the declaration by which Jesus taught, proved, and attested, even unto death, His divine Sonship; after having examined and re-cognised the unassailable value of His testimony, we have by that very fact obtained a reasonable right to believe in the Divinity of Jesus. Note that phrase: the right to believe. We do not believe anyhow. In order to believe we must have the right, and not the duty only. In this case the right precedes the duty; no one can believe unless he has the right to believe; and the right is conferred on him by reason.

This may seem a strange saying, but it is absolutely certain. If not, we must conclude, to the shame of belief, that faith is arbitrary, and may be refused at our pleasure, while it becomes a right and a duty for whomsoever has examined and accepted the title-deeds offered by faith.

It therefore would seem that all those who have taken serious account of the belief in the Divinity of Jesus must accept this fact—this transcendent truth. Nothing of the kind. For man has the power of refusing his adhesion even to things attested by credible witnesses—a formidable power, which he uses, or rather abuses.

At the present day, many who have given their attention to this important truth, that Jesus has declared His divine Sonship, who have recognised, by a sincere and rational examination, that they ought to accept the declaration of Jesus, yet refuse to acquiesce in this declared truth, violate a duty, withdrawing from a right which they will not use, although they are to blame for not using it.

I often wonder—I say this in all the frankness of my faith and all the simplicity of my nature, in spite of the experience I have gained of the contradictions and rebellions of the human conscience—I often wonder that these men are able to withdraw themselves so easily from faith in the Divinity of Jesus. And to my astonishment is added bitter sadness; for to the heart of an upright man nothing can be more grievous than to see a truth, which is manifest to all eyes, disdained, misunderstood, and rejected. However, whoso reflects on what the Divinity of

Jesus implies, and the act of faith which it demands, and on the very nature of reason, is less inclined to wonder at the facility with which man refuses to believe.

There are two sorts of truth : those we can demonstrate by intrinsic evidence, and those we can demonstrate extrinsically. The former are clear; the second remain, in spite of their manifest credibility, in the shade of mystery. In the first the evidence is such that the intellect is vanquished and bound in subjection; men cannot but accept them.

You show me in science a visible fact—I accept it without discussion ; or you prove an assertion by a syllogism which allows me to seize accurately the conclusions involved in its premisses, and the syllogism has all the clearness of the evidence : in these conditions the reason acts for itself, and acquiesces deliberately, without resistance.

But it is otherwise when a truth wherein the intrinsic evidence is not given—as, for example, the Divine Sonship of Jesus. A witness, Jesus Himself, declares it, confirming it by evident exterior signs ; but if this witness and these signs give it credibility they do not prove it. Now, human intelligence being only convinced and overcome by evidence, what I am about to say will explain one of the general causes of the

K

unbelief of many. In such a case the will must
come in, overmaster our minds, and say to the
reason : " Restrain thyself ; here is a witness
who speaks ; He speaks truly ; bow thyself down,
in spite of the mystery which enfolds the reality
whereof He testifies."

In certain cases, then, evidence is supreme, in
others testimony. In this case, the will must
sway the intellect, because the witness is
credible ; but if the will does not bear sway,
faith will not exist. Now the will of a large
number does not command the assent of reason ;
hence unbelief in regard to the Divinity of Jesus ;
and this is an interesting phenomenon which we
must study. If the will remain inert, it must be
paralysed and rendered immovable by some
obstacle. The difficulties which paralyse and
check human will and intellect in regard to
belief depend upon three causes : the intrinsic
cause is the act of faith itself ; the next, which
I will call subjective, depends on the subject, on
his psychological, intellectual, and moral state ;
the third, which I will call general and extrinsic,
is the conditions in which the subject lives, and
whose influences press on him on every side.

Persuaded that when these difficulties are
known they are half overcome, I proceed to
examine with you, one after the other, the
obstacles which hinder us from giving our

adhesion to belief in the Divinity of Jesus, Son of God and Son of Man.

The first source of the difficulties opposed to faith is the act of faith itself.

If in believing we had nothing to do but to formulate with our lips the dogma that Jesus is the Son of Man and Son of God, the matter would be very simple. If we had even to formulate it in our minds it would still be very simple. But the act of faith goes further ; it draws with it the whole human being, and applies it altogether to the truth of which it is the object.

In fact, since the will commands the intellect to acquiesce in the fact that the divinity was in Jesus, will comes into play. And, as will can only act under the sway of reason, which has demonstrated the credibility of testimony, the intellect has also an essential part in the act of faith.

The two great faculties of the human being are therefore put in movement. Yet more : when the intellect, moved by the will, accepts this truth that Jesus is the Son of God, such an adhesion carries with it grave and important consequences.

In fact, if Jesus is truly the Son of God, and we recognise Him as such, then by that very fact we submit entirely to Him. We give ourselves a Master in the intellectual order, in the order ot thought, because it is evident that if the Son of God speak we must listen.   We give ourselves a Master in the order of the will, because if the Son of God give us precepts we must follow them.   We give ourselves a Master in the order of the affections, because if the Son of God be there we must love Him, love Him as He deserves, with an altogether sovereign love.   We give ourselves a Master in the order of activity, because if He command our wills, our affections, and our emotions, nothing more remains.   Intellect, will, affection and emotion comprise the whole of human activity.

Now, we must understand the meaning of those words : " to give ourselves a Master."   It is to belong no more to self.   Now nothing is harder and more contrary to a man who understands himself, who has his own will and feels himself the master of his actions, of his thoughts and of his will; the master of his emotions, his activity—in a word, of his whole being.

Therefore, when the will refuses to enforce on the intellect the act of faith in the Divinity of Jesus Christ, we may be quite sure that the first cause of this refusal is the secret and unacknowledged fear of submitting to a master.   Man instinctively desires to be his own master.   He does not willingly bow to another sovereign.   He declares that thought is his own, that will is his own, that he can love and act as he pleases; he declines to think, to will, to love, and to act under the influence and empire of another. This age, wherein the sense of individualism is so strong—I might even say so excessive—is no time to speak of the difficulties of belief, and yet I cannot ignore them. We have all felt them: we are all framed of the same clay, we all breathe the same air, we all have the same passions and the same inclinations; and, since there is at the present day a fever of independence, none can declare that he has never felt some access of it. Even among believers there is none whose belief is reasoned and convinced, who has not felt that the act of belief implies a painful renunciation.

You know what ancient slavery was. The soul of a modern man cannot contain his indignation, revolt, and anger against the times when slavery bore so heavily on two-thirds of humanity, with the approbation even of philosophers, who regarded it as natural and necessary. Yet in spite of his chains and in spite of the material servitude which weighed upon his body, the slave was able to keep his soul free. While you who believe in Jesus Christ keep the liberty of your members, you can go and come where you please; but the Divine Master takes something away from you—He takes away the autonomy of conscience. Yes, Christian, you

may come and go, you may do externally what
your will and even your caprice dictates, so only
that morality does not hinder you ; but you
cannot think what your intellectual caprice
chooses, nor will what your desire suggests, nor
love in all the independence of a fickle heart ; you
cannot move in the order of activity where interest
comes into play, without Christ rising to confront
you, without the Son of God stating with absolute
sovereignty what you ought to think, what you
ought to love, what you ought to will, what you
ought to do.   Unlike the slave of antiquity, your
body is free, your soul is in chains.   That is the
act of faith, in its grave austerity, in the grandeur
of its sacrifice.

When the Christian has done this, not with his
mere lips, as those who seem to believe, and in
reality believe no more than heathens ; but with
full consciousness and will, he can repeat the word
of St. Paul : " I live, not now I, but Christ liveth
in me." There is not a true believer who has not
sacrificed himself, who is not a slave of Jesus, the
Son of God ; a sublime slave, no doubt, but still a
slave, and we who carry a free soul before men,
take a pride in this boast of slavery, and feel an
enthusiasm which the most independent freedman,
drunk with liberty, has never known.

It avails me nothing to be my own master if I
am a tyrant to myself.   What I ask is to be the

slave of truth and universal good. Oh, Christ, when Thou didst demand our faith, Thou didst enter into us with the truth that bears sway over the mind, and I adore Thee ; with that eternal good which is the law of the will, and I adore Thee again ; with love, the eternal love which God alone knows, and I adore Thee for evermore. What matters it that I exist no longer ? what matters it to me that our wretched self should be immolated ; I glorify that sacrifice where the individual renounces himself, escapes from his own limits and his own nothingness, sacrificing himself to belong thenceforward only to eternal truth, eternal goodness, and eternal love.

This is the first difficulty in believing. I feel the difficulty most intimately, and I am full of compassion for those poor unbelievers who turn away from the light. I know them well as they shrink from the sacrificial pyre ; it is but human to do so. Believers would fain fling themselves into the holy flames : a beautiful and heroic sacrifice. In every one who believes in the Son of God there are the makings of a hero. I do not say in all believers. Of all religious masters, Jesus is the only one who has the right to ask for this heroism ; for, being the Son of God, He is truth and love and the absolute good. But no human slavery finds a sanction among believers. There is not a single chain which will find amongst us even the

smallest hammer to forge it.   We leave chains to
slave-dealers.

Slave for slave I prefer to those who are slaves
to themselves, or to the crowd of humanity, the
proud and gentle slaves of God.

We see, then, what are the inherent difficulties
in the very act of faith ; I may point out to you
others not less grave and not less dangerous, the
result of our psychological, intellectual, and moral
state.

If we consider the present state of men and
of minds, we find them divided into four categories :

The first comprises those who live, or think they
live, by the mind—those who think, or believe that
they think, among whom the brain is preponderant ; the second, those in whom the heart bears
sway ; the third, those whom material activity
masters and absorbs ; workmen of every degree
and every class, from the civil engineer to the
humble and obscure miner ; and the fourth, those
who are swayed by passion and follow their more
or less unruly instincts.   These four categories sum
up the whole mass of humanity.

Now, on whichever I look, I see special and
dangerous difficulties to the act of faith in the
Divinity of Jesus Christ.

Look first at those who think, or believe that
they think.   I put on one side all really great

minds. I will not here quote them or argue with them : their measure is beyond mine. Since they tower above the level of ordinary humanity, we can scarcely, even in these democratic days of equality, address such majestic beings. I take the average, that is to say, those who have the culture of their times, those whose brain attains to the level of modern civilisation.

Now, these have a great difficulty in the act of faith, and the secret reason is that they all have, or think they have, a little rational system, varying with the individual. In some it is a scepticism more or less transcendent, more or less logical, analytic and experimental; in others it is idealism, in others pantheism, in others positivism, in others blank materialism, in others—what shall I say ? Nothing, nothing ! As soon as anything is affirmed, they fly off ; they have a horror of affirmation, they abstain from committing themselves, and this abstention, systematised, is called Agnosticism.

Now the system in which such minds are encased is by no means the result of profound study. They merely seek what suits them, and take it as they would take a hat at a hatter's. When you have to do with minds who are so provided with some such a system, it is not possible to bring them to any active faith.

These theories, in fact, are just the negation of

all faith ; you dash against a wall, or fire against a cuirass which your bullet cannot penetrate. All struggle is impossible ; no faith can triumph over this very general state of mind.

I do not think that I exaggerate in speaking thus : experience gives me proof that this diseased state of mind comes on a man before he has reached his thirtieth year ; it may even arise about the twentieth, even before ; according to physiology, the sutures are completely closed and the physical man is complete.

Yet more ; besides those minds which do not go so far as to provide themselves with a system, there are those who fall under the yoke of the intellectual prejudices of their time. The irreligious prejudice betrays itself by aphorisms such as these : Science has demonstrated that miracles are impossible ; science has shown that we are the descendants of apes ; science proves that all creation is an irresistible and fatal evolution of matter. Among political prejudices we hear the following : The priest is a useless being, he had better retire to his sacristy that we may see him no longer ; he should conceal himself behind his churches and no longer thwart us in the material order, which it is ours to keep, with which, moreover, he has nothing to do, for his kingdom is not of this world.

It cannot be denied that such prejudices blind

and narrow the minds of those who claim to live
by thought, and they raise between themselves
and faith an impenetrable and unbroken wall of
China. And when we have placed before the eyes
of these blind men irresistible testimony, when we
have proved that Jesus attested His divinity, and
that the testimony of Jesus ought to be received,
they remain deaf and blind; hearing they do not
hear; seeing they do not see; they remain fixed
in their prejudices and their theory as if you
talked Chinese to an European.

Believe, however, that in spite of the severity of
my language, I feel as a priest a profound com-
miseration for those far from the faith, who suffer
the grievous slavery of their vain systems and their
prejudices.

May youth especially learn how to free itself
from them. In the name of liberty which it
worships, of the frankness in which it glories, in
the name of that great, simple Catholic reason
which lights up with all its powerful rays, may it
free itself from all yokes and break them in
pieces; one only Master is worthy of it, Christ.
May it find at His feet its best inspiration and its
divine Saviour.

Those who live by their hearts are differently
placed, and face to face with other difficulties
which I must now point out.

The heart of man tends to idolise the object of

its affections; so all who live by the heart, unless
they allow themselves to be governed by a superior
wisdom, are necessarily dragged into an idolatry of
the affections which is one of the great facts of
our human nature.   Women who hear me will be
able to testify to the truth of my words.

When a man is carried away by feeling, he is
absorbed in his object, seeing nothing beyond,
beneath, or above it.   It is a sort of enchantment which leaves no liberty of thought, of will,
or of act; and those who are thus constrained
and enchanted are true slaves, most unhappy and
most cruelly treated.

If, indeed, the idol which we have made could
give back all that with which we endow it; but
the idol is of marble or of bronze, it is of iron or
steel; let it be of gold or of living flesh, if you will,
it is still an idol; and the idol has always reduced
to servitude, degraded and devoured those who
adore it.

Such in sober sadness is the history of those
who are carried away by love.   They are led like
unresisting sheep.   It is impossible to escape the
magic wand which leads them, bleeding and en-
chained, whither the fancy of the master takes
them.   Man is not a volcano that his heart should
break out and carry everything before it.   Our
emotions ought to have a natural law as the
instincts of a beast have.   Feeling has in it some-

thing infinite, and when it turns to the creature, it clothes it with the infinite which is in him, but not in the creature; he makes it into a divinity. Now, every creature which is made into a divinity is but an idol, and all idols are men-slayers and slayers of their brethren, as cruel as they are debauched. A multitude of men are given over, in different degrees, to the violence of unbridled human passion. There are two millions of inhabitants in Paris, and if you could look into the consciences you would see how large a flock is driven by the scourge of frantic love. They are happy in their unconsciousness of the lash, happy in the whirlwind which overwhelms them. But when they come to themselves they shrink in terror before the reality of facts. The mind revolts, they do not know where they are going; they go forward to the unknown, always attracted and always deceived, intoxicated and unappeased. They are mad.

If you try to speak to them of God and of the Divinity of Jesus, or to bring them back to the faith, you might as well speak to sleep-walkers and hypnotised persons.

You can no more influence a world like this than that of minds blinded with prejudice and fortified by systems. They are scattered here and there, but we have all known a few. The character which always marks them is that of madness. If you speak to them of God, they have only one god, that is the loved one; you speak to them of conscience, there is only one conscience for them, the voice which tells them what they must do for that they love; and so the crowd of desperate men is recruited.

Consult your own personal experience. When they have not been overwhelmed by the fire which devours them, when they have escaped the burning furnace into which they have thrown themselves, when they fluttered out half consumed, their despair has no words. If God is not there to help these natures whose last fibres are broken, you hear the sad echo of those terrible dramas which make you shudder.

Our modern civilisation, developing to excess the emotional nature, has also multiplied to excess the number of these victims, incurable, though the flame has not yet reduced them to ashes. We are unable, alas! to save them, and see them fluttering and dying; and this is one of the most terrible obstacles to the hold of faith in the human soul.

Hearts which are in bondage to the creature, wrapped up and possessed by the love of the creature, are closed to God.

Jesus passes them by, afar off; leaving them to the despair which ruin has already begun; leaves them to their madness, the last crime of prostituted humanity which will not seek eternal love.

There are also in our present world those whom we call men of action, great and little alike. Now men of action are carried away by the torrent of earthly activity.

You know our modern society, and can realise all the agitations, preoccupations, and feverish impatience which it contains. The man of our day dreams of colossal enterprises, and his dreams consume him; he thinks of nothing but how to change the whole surface of our planet, altering its conditions, bringing about a new order of things, becoming the master of Nature, taming her forces, suppressing time and space. And such a work as this demands workmen. For you cannot annihilate distance without the combined and persevering effort of thousands of workmen. And here is the strange irony of things! the humblest are as necessary as the greatest, and those who themselves are the most stationary—the miners in their caves—beget the force which gives the impulse to the colossal machine; if you eliminate them, all is stopped.

From the entrails of the earth they extract the consolidated rays of the sun, just as we extract the honeycomb from the hive. But the absorption and exhaustion of their daily task is terrible. Those whom this form of incessant and overwhelming labour consumes can think of nothing else. Bowed towards the earth and sunk in its depth, they cannot look up to God.

At the end of their long and exhausting day, they hardly can gain any rest in their families, with their sons and daughters ; they drop with fatigue in the evening, after an excess of labour. And we ask what at such a moment is able to upraise their souls and revive their courage ?

If they look at the fire crackling on the hearth —if there be a fire ; the fortunate among them have always a fire, but many have not—it revives at the moment when it seemed to be going out. If they lift their eyes above they will see, above the chimneypiece, above the hearth, another flame—that which comes from the Crucifix—the protector of Christian hearths.

But in order to look there, they must have that traditional faith which is guarded as a sacred patrimony ; and too frequently they have lost it, and are incapable of finding it again, so many are the difficulties and the obstacles around them which hinder their belief.

Even men of letters rarely attain to this faith ; and, that being so, how shall those who are without culture, those whose only enlightenment is derived from the halfpenny papers, find the means of belief, and the secret of uplifting their weary consciences, even more weary than their exhausted arms ?

I know the attempts to give them amusement. But if we have succeeded in withdrawing them for a moment from the torrent which sweeps them along, these poor wretches soon fall under the yoke of their misery and their labour, and this crushing yoke cannot give them the courage to be workmen without reproach, wise and prudent fathers of families, able to increase their salaries by thrift, in order that at the critical hour they may heal their children and heal themselves.

Good God! This is the truth of the social situation : the workman needs faith, and his hard life takes from him the possibility of it.

In speaking thus, I am not thinking only of the proletariat, of the weak brethren, those who are visibly oppressed by the woes of the body. I speak also for the great, the intellectual, and the strong; and they will pardon me if I take pity on them as I do on the others. Their sorrow is equally dark, though it be hidden under the brightness of triumphant activity; it offers even less hold to the priest who endeavours to bring them the word of Christ, apart from which they seek in vain the God of all power and all hope, the God of consolation and of peace.

I am sure you agree with me, and, bestowing on all those absorbed in the active affairs of life a common compassion, you would wish for the lowest

L

workman or the highest engineer the knowledge how to live the life of the soul in the midst of the din of the world, the devouring activity which draws the soul far from God and condemns it to death.

There is, in our world of to-day, as in all the states of civilisation which have preceded it, the category of those who are carried away by their instincts, who are governed neither by mind nor by feeling, who are not wrapped up in the hurry of business, but whom a sort of whirlwind of passion seizes and leads captive. I speak of the mere human beast—forgive me such an expression —a beast which has not raised itself or which has not been raised to the heights of reason, of will and of enlightened interest.

In our civilisation this category is especially developed in great cities. Humanity, like the sea, has its foam and its wreckage. I may add, moreover, that those beings who are given over to brutal instincts, if they be but a little refined, easily take their place in society, wear a mask which prevents our recognising them.

Well, this human beast is refractory, is uncongenial to faith in the divinity of Jesus and to everything which is noble. "The animal man," says St. Paul, "cannot understand the things of God."

Here too lies hid a bottomless misery. Into

those dark and gaping abysses we must look
when we wish to fathom all that is inferior, gross,
perverse, and violent in poor humanity. Speci-
mens are, alas! so numerous that it is easy to
examine the phenomenon. The faith of Christ
cannot spring up in those souls consumed by the
fire of earth, nor can the light of God shine in
this impenetrable darkness. At the last moment,
it is true, we are occasionally able to save these
beings reduced to the last degree of moral corruption whom infinite mercy wills to recover.

We may say perhaps that we ought to take no
account of these, but the priests of Jesus, who
know the divine value of souls, can never treat the
lowest among them as a negligeable quantity, and
I am not alone in thinking thus; all those who
possess the heart of an apostle would be glad to
try, even at the peril of their life, to tame these
degraded natures who are all the more wretched
that they often have not the consciousness of their
baseness and their misery.

In any case we have here the sign of the inherent corruption of humanity. It may be said
that these beings do not belong to humanity, and
that they have not risen out of their mere animal
nature, but I for my part consider that they have
gone back to it.

Now it is just this that we ought to prevent.
The legislator should not ever seek only to punish;

he should attempt prevention.   He should not be like those who wake on a sudden at the onset of danger to aid those who cry : Help ! help ! True soldiers have other tactics. Defence is good, but to prevent attack is better. In a great country like ours, this is the urgent duty, and while I utter no reproach against those who have the honour to rule it, I permit myself in my independence as a priest to offer them a word of advice. I would say to them : Destroy in the germ the human animal which may be a danger to the society of which you have the care. It lies with you to prevent cata-strophes.

And I would add : Take care of morals—an old precept which people do not care for now— old, because eternal.

The chief care of those in power should not be the vigorous assault on evil, but the development of those healthy and unseen influences, whereby the reason which is inherent in civilisation, and the morality which makes law, penetrate little by little into the conscience of the lowest and the soul of the most insignificant.

I dare not say whether our rulers do this or not, and I leave it to your own reason and your impartial wisdom to answer.

I cannot leave the subject which I have wished to treat in your presence without once more calling your attention to the surroundings in which we all live and which oppose great difficulties to faith in God and belief in the Divinity of Jesus, which two things are really one and the same.

I shall not be suspected of darkening the picture of my time ; I am ready to declare that I love it more than any other century, for the simple reason that I belong to it, just as a man loves his own family more than other families because it is his own ; and this reason, which springs from the heart, is always accepted and suffers no contradiction.

Among all the sorrows of our time, there is a very characteristic one which I will venture to call by the name of the atrophy of the religious sense.

Humanity obeys three kinds of influence : the influence of earth, from which we can never free ourselves; the human influence of our surroundings, which we cannot escape ; and, lastly, the superior and divine influence, which constitutes the better part of man.

If the feet of man are firmly planted on the earth ; if his breast dilates as it fills with the air which surrounds it ; his brain takes in the world, and he feels by his very attitude that the earth is not all, that those who surround him are only a part of what is real, and that the world really has its centre beyond his vision, higher than earth, higher than humanity.

Now that which characterises our age is, on the one hand, the energetic development of the force by which we put matter in motion and of the activity by which we influence society for its own perfection; and, on the other, the languor and feebleness of the movement with which we tend towards God.

I am grieved at this, and others with me. And yet we may not despair. Man is not a complete being. Among the children of the Heavenly Father each one has his own physiognomy; some are well born, others less so; some have physical strength, others the poetic genius to sing of Nature; some have their heads bowed down better to see their earthly road, others look up and adore.

The centuries succeed each other and differ each from the other; we must take them as they are, without holding a brief for them. I defend my own only in part; I recognise the predominant tendency of those who guide its course; they are concerned with the problems of matter or towards social questions, and I find that this movement offers a difficulty to the belief in the Divinity of Jesus Christ.

For this very reason that if we were less engaged, less busy, we should better feel the attraction of what is divine; now this attraction is revealed in Jesus, and those who do not feel the thirst for the divine pass by Him, distracted and indifferent.

I would remind you of it. It does appeal to me, you will say; but I, who am devoured by this thirst, rush to Him as we run to a fount of living water. You will recognise that men like him who speaks to you being in the minority, the masses turn themselves to social, economic, colonial, and international questions, to all which touch human interests. They are engaged in piercing tunnels, making railways, constructing such or such works as seem to you very fine; for example, the submarine tunnel, or a gigantic bridge in the open air, between France and England. But when you say to men who are doing these things: "Look towards God," they answer you: "We have neither time nor inclination to do so."

We, however, who, in the midst of this torrent which carries us all towards matter, have kept the hunger and thirst for God, we go to God; and when the testimonies of God are heard, we bow down ourselves in an act of faith and say: "O Christ, I adore Thee, since Thou givest me the God whom I sought."

Yet we know that men pass unmoved by the side of that which is a passion with us, hurrying madly onward without a suspicion of that living fount from which we draw courage to undertake and to endure all.

Such is our age. Faith does not reign therein in a full stream as do science and democracy, but this need not dismay us. Time passes, and there is room under God's sun for all the acts of the great drama which is transacted in humanity.

At the present day men are not drawn in the direction in which we would fain see them go. We must gather up the greatest number that we can without anathematising those who withdraw themselves from us, and we must wait for better times with the patience of God whom we represent, and of Jesus who has sent us to bear witness to Him.

Fear nothing, and recognise even in this age in which we live, under a grey, sometimes a darkened sky, without sun in the day, without stars in the night, the power of Him of whom I preach to you.

In this night of the end of the nineteenth century, against this night of God, against the murky sky—a sky darkened by the thick dust raised by human toil—you may see the great Church of God arise and stand. It is the column of fire which tells you that light has not gone out. When men, too much occupied with earth and with themselves, darken the world, there always remains to guide them on their road and to show them the good, the eternal light of God shining through the darkness of humanity, as stars shine through the clouds of heaven.

VII

THE SEVEN WORDS OF JESUS ON THE CROSS

I INTERRUPT to-day the course of my lectures, for we have come together to-day to celebrate the anniversary of the death of Jesus Christ.

This death is the most important fact in the annals of humanity; that which most deeply stirs our grief and our emotion, and yet it is the most consoling and the most powerful. Nothing can be compared with it.

In fact the death of Jesus Christ and the cross which was its instrument divided human history into two parts—the one which preceded, the other which followed that event—and these two parts resemble each other in nothing; they are in absolute contradiction one with the other, and it is the cross of Jesus which has produced this contradiction, an honour to humanity and altogether to our advantage.

The death of Jesus, and His passion—passion which cannot be expressed in words, is the divine coronation of His life. All that He taught and manifested to us, all the examples of virtue which He gave, all the weariness which He endured, all the treasures of wisdom, love, power, and goodness which He manifested, are concentrated in His last hour.

His death was not that of a man, it was that of a God. Let those who seek to believe contemplate it ; and, as it drew from the Roman centurion that immortal cry from an upright conscience : " Indeed this was the Son of God ! " it will, after all these centuries, win from all sincere souls the same cry and the same faith.

I cannot repress the emotion which I feel when I speak to you as a disciple speaks of his Master. Eighteen hundred and ninety-four years ago at this same moment—the sixth hour, as it was called at that time—on the little bare hill which was called the place of a skull, Jesus was raised on the cross. I see the place, I see the ancient ramparts of Jerusalem as it then was ; I see the angle formed by the wall which sloped away from a defensive tower called the Tower of Hippicus, which went direct to a gate, the Gate Djennat ; I see another wall starting at a right angle from the gate and running due north. There, some twenty paces from the walls—for it was the custom to execute those comdemned to death at the gates of the town —there, some twenty paces off, near the road which

went to Ephraim of Samaria, in the midst of the
olive gardens where the rich Israelites dug their
tombs, in the midst of a crowd, Jesus, accompanied by two brigands, thieves, or malefactors,
was crucified.

Now there fell from the divine lips of Jesus on
the cross, words which were recorded by those who
heard them; we are here to meditate upon them,
and I would wish to explain them to you; poor
explanation, however, beside all the infinite depths
which those words contain.

Oh, my brethren, the dying Jesus left us the
great knowledge of life in those few words which
fell from His lips, and the knowledge of life is the
knowledge of suffering, is the knowledge of woe,
of consolation, affection, and of pardon. It is the
knowledge of perfection—in one word it is the
knowledge of how to die.

There is one word which teaches the rudiments
of this divine knowledge, the most necessary to
man, for we may be ignorant of everything, my
brethren, in this world except one thing, the
knowledge of how to die. Now, the first word
which fell from the lips of Jesus is a word of
pardon: "Father, forgive them, for they know
not what they do," He said as He was raised on
the cross, speaking of His executioners.

We all suffer, more or less, by the deeds of men:
their ill-will and their antipathy, their violence or

their craft, their secret hostility or their open persecution. Although born to love each other as
brethren, men tear each other in pieces. The
sorrow caused by unconscious nature, the sorrow
inherent in our fragile constitution, is more easy to
bear; we resign ourselves to it of necessity, as to
inexorable fate; but the sorrow which comes from
an intelligent and free cause, from those among
whom we live, our fellow-citizens, our friends and
our relatives, that is the sorrow which is most
excruciating of all, a terrible sorrow, especially
when it follows upon an innocent person who has
the right to say to his enemies : " Why do you
persecute me ? "   Jesus did not even make this
reproach to His executioners; He forgave them
fully, simply. Let us say as He did and with
Him : " Father, forgive them, for they know not
what they do ! "

We look for this word from Christ. He had
always taught forgiveness; He had recommended
it as His new law, and had said to His disciples :
" They will persecute you, but do you bless them;
they will insult you, do and say what is good;
love your enemies. Pardon without counting, not
seven times, but seventy times seven, that is,
always."

And now, Master, here is Thy supreme hour.
What wilt Thou do upon the Cross to which Thou
art nailed by Thine enemies ?   Thou wilt forgive.

From the hour of this forgiveness an immense pity has developed the earth; the victims have learnt to curse no longer, but to forgive and to love. Forgiveness! Not only did Jesus call for pardon, but He asked it from His Father for His executioners; and He added, thus giving the secret of infinite mercy : " Forgive them, for they know not what they do."

Now notice that when man does evil, it is always at bottom from ignorance. Man does not know. No doubt his will has its weaknesses, its obstinacies, and aberrations; but an attentive examination of conscience shows that they proceed, most of them, from ignorance of the mind. Man's intellect is very short; he does not see or understand, and therefore he errs. The executioners who crucified Jesus would certainly not have crucified Him if they had known what He was. Their ignorance excuses them and opens a side door to infinite mercy.

Now see the effect of this divine word. Humanity, considered in regard to God, is ruled by two laws—that of Justice, which strikes and avenges; that of Mercy, which absolves and loves.

Jesus lived under the law of avenging Justice, under the law of the terrible Jehovah, which left no place in human conscience for goodness and forgiveness. Inflexible humanity seized the sword, struck and slew, armed with that false justice which is called *lex talionis.* It was a formidable law, which had dominion in the whole world before Jesus. After Him this law was changed; since He pronounced the word of for-giveness a new spirit has taken possession of the heart of man. We are kind, even to weakness; but we need not excuse ourselves too much. We may be well permitted to imitate our God, and to have for the bad a cry of pity. In the kingdom of Jesus there is no more vengeance, no more reprisals, no more killing, no swords brandished to intimidate the human beast. We must imitate Jesus; and even when the claws of the human brute pierce our flesh, we must contain our wrath, open our hearts to pity, and not withdraw ourselves from this outpouring of the forgiveness of God.

O my Lord! blessed art Thou, for Thou hast changed what was most difficult to change in man. Thou hast slain the instinct of vengeance, and brought about the reign of mercy and of boundless pardon.

If to pronounce the word of forgiveness, even in favour of the executioner, belongs to the heroism of man, to create in the heart of hu-manity the divine law of universal mercy belongs to God alone.

Jesus was crucified between two brigands,

thieves, or murderers. The second word which
fell from His lips was a word of the most touching consolation. One of those crucified with Him
joined with the general crowd, with the passers-
by, the Pharisees, the Jewish authorities, all
vying with each other in insulting the Crucified,
and said: " If thou be Christ, save Thyself and
us." He continued his evil life even in his death;
but the other, rebuking the companion of his
punishment, said, in all the sincerity of his soul:
" We receive the due reward of our deeds, but
this man hath done no evil." Then looking upon
Jesus he said to him: " Lord, remember me, when
Thou shalt come into Thy kingdom." Jesus
answered him: " This day thou shalt be with Me
in Paradise."

My brethren, I know no word that is better
addressed to the whole of humanity. All we here
are, in our different degrees, sinners. I do not
say that we have been robbers, thieves, assassins,
as any man who is the victim of public wrath, or
as they who, condemned by Pilate, went with
Jesus to His death; but we have our vices, and
we are sometimes more culpable than those who
are declared malefactors, more criminal than
murderers. Some men kill the body, but others
corrupt the spirit and slay the soul. Of these
two crimes, which is the greatest in the sight of
God? Intellectual malefactors! you have perhaps

distilled into a whole generation your evil venom.
Race of vipers! it is not a single man whom you
have morally slain, but thousands of men; and as
for the corrupters, the perverse, they have cor-
rupted a thousand consciences and sowed shame
and incurable vice in many families. They drape
themselves in their decorous civilisation, and
speak of virtue in order to make us believe in
their own; and they have the insolence of self-
admiration under their hypocritical mask.

We will have no illusion, no deception, and no
sham. Human conscience faints under the burden
of innumerable crimes open or secret. And,
strange though it be, the most innocent before God
recognise and publish with the highest frankness
and sincerity their sins and woes.

My brethren, you cannot escape death, which
lies in wait for you. I do not say that we have
to be nailed to a cross, but we shall certainly be
nailed to the bed of death and draw our last
breath.

And you who listen to me, what need you for
that tragic hour? What do I need, above all, who
speak to you here? We need hope; for that
which takes strongest hold of the human being
when in the hour of death he has a vivid sense of
his own unworthiness, that which tortures him
and often renders his salvation impossible, is the
leaven of despair which rises suddenly in us. And

at the end of a long life, when in the mournful gloom of death we examine our actions, we are inclined to say: " Leave me; I am too far from God. Let me die, and make an end of it."

This is the bitter cry of the desperate, and I would wish that you should have once for all the remedy against that supreme anguish. Look at that nameless wretch who died by the side of Jesus! He was a criminal like those of to-day, for times, like evil actions, scarcely change. Civilisations are modified, but the essence of evil is always identical and its fruits of death are always similar.

I would address myself in the name of Jesus, in the name of the Crucified, the great, the only Consoler, to all those who are unhappy because they are sinful—and we are never absolutely unhappy unless we are sinful—I would address myself to those who have made publc failure of honour, those who have made failure in the secret of their conscience; those who have made failure in their passion, failed in the law, failed in regard to society, I would say to all these criminals—to all, you understand, for they are all on the same road, and breathe the same atmosphere of Satanic evil: whoever you are, whatever be the number and the greatness of your crimes, never despair. Young women who have fallen, do not despair; faithless wives, do not despair; husbands bowed

M

down under the weight of secret shame, do not despair; you who are perjured to all oaths, oppressors of the weak, traitors to justice, enemies of religion, blasphemers of God, do not despair, for since Jesus said to him who was crucified with Him: "To-day thou shalt be with me in Paradise," despair is conquered. Paradise is God, Paradise is truth, Paradise is eternal love ; Paradise is infinite power, Paradise is perfection; it is the kingdom of God, it is eternal justice and eternal love.

Such is the dream to which we cling in the fulness of our higher instincts and of our most sublime aspirations. Paradise is the hope of the sinner ; Jesus promises it to him.

Brethren, one thing is to be done to obtain Paradise, and that depends upon yourselves : to smite your breasts and return into your own consciences, to pronounce that word from the depths of your heart in the example and with the faith of the good thief : " I have done ill, and I have received the punishment which I ought to receive, but Thou, O Jesus, art innocent; remember me, when Thou comest into Thy kingdom."

And may all you who hear me learn this lesson, when you feel your sins weigh heavily upon you, when despair threatens to overwhelm you, look to the eternal Calvary and say to Him who is dying there : " When Thou comest into Thy kingdom— and Thou art there now—remember me !"

Oh, my brethren, would that I could wring from you this cry; that I could bring home to your troubled consciences—I do not say into your dead consciences, but, what is worse, your despairing consciences—the saving word. Yes, you will hear it with the thief on Calvary, the word of Christ, the secret of eternal consolation : " This day thou shalt be with me in Paradise."

At the foot of the Cross a scene took place, most moving because most human. The soul of Jesus was therein revealed in its exquisite and infinite tenderness. Round those who were crucified there was a surging crowd, curious to see them, full of ill-will and evil dispositions. The greater number of them were mocking, threatening and ironical, full of insults and blasphemies against Jesus. A little apart stood in silent grief the holy women who had accompanied Jesus in His mission.

One moment the mother of Jesus, her sister-in-law Mary, the wife of Cleophas, John the well-beloved disciple, and Mary Magdalene, drawn by an invincible attraction, came near, in spite of danger, as though to mingle their anguish with the anguish of the Crucified. Jesus saw His mother, He saw the beloved disciple, His eyes rested on them with unspeakable tenderness ; He forgot His pain to think only of those whom He loved, for if there is one trait more remarkable than any other in His life, and in particular during His passion, it was the forgetfulness of His own grief.

From the moment when He left the Prætorium and met the women of Jerusalem manifesting by their wailing, according to Oriental custom, the immense pity of the people, down to the last hour wherein he gave His soul into the hands of the Father, Jesus forgot Himself; so different to the man who concentrates himself in his own woe, and in suffering thinks of nothing but his own pain. Great is the lesson and austere the teaching—no egotism, especially in suffering; you should endure it, forget it and forget yourself, after the example of Jesus on Calvary, nailed to the Cross, resting His eyes on the group of those whom He loved most in the world—His mother, John his friend, Mary Cleophas the friend of his mother, and Mary Magdalene, His penitent — His affection poured itself forth on them for the last time before His death.

He uttered some wonderful words, admirably human ; He made as it were His testament. You will understand this, you who have seen any beloved being die, and treasured up his last wishes ; He looked at His mother and John, then He said to His mother : " Woman, behold thy son," and to John, " Behold thy mother."

Jesus, seeing death take Him from his mother,

not being able any more to be visibly the Son
of Mary, He gave her His most beloved apostle
John as a son in His place; John was to watch
over her, and the mother of Jesus was to watch
over the disciple whom He loved. Being no longer
able to lie on the breast of the Master, John would
live at least near her who had been with Him all
His life, from His conception to His death, and in
hearing the beatings of the Mother's heart he
would find in them the echo of all the divine
mysteries which he would translate to the world
in his sublime Gospel; that Gospel which is an
offence to those whose minds cannot endure to
contemplate the high things of God, and whose
hearts harden themselves before His infinite pity.

Such in its simplicity was the testament of Jesus.
We Christians have always seen in it a profound
and touching symbol. Its tender humanity conceals a touching mystery, and, from the beginning,
all those who have been initiated into the doctrine
of Christ have seen there a great creation of the
dying Jesus; the creation of a spiritual and universal Motherhood of which Mary would be the
organ, and a spiritual sonship embracing all the
disciples of Jesus represented by John.

Women will ponder on this wonderful height to
which it has pleased Jesus to raise them in the
person of her who is at the head of their sex, and,
after Christ, even at the head of humanity. I here

reveal to you a great mystery of Providence, and however respectful may be my auditors, I feel a certain scruple—I would not profane holy things and give the truth of God to be trampled by the feet of those who disdain it.

Must we then go into the desert to escape the lightness and the irony of men, and in the desert call together the initiated to tell them in the tranquillity of solitude and the respect of their conscience the holy truths of which we are the depositories? No, O Christ Jesus! Thou hast willed, in accepting Thy Cross, to be exposed to the world, and in Thy divine nakedness to be the mark for every form of insult, and we must bear them with Thee. In the spiritual and divine order as Providence has established it on earth, we have not only a Redeemer who communicates to us the spirit and grace of God, we have not only a Master and a Father, we have a Mother, and her name is Mary; and since she has been raised to this divine position, she certainly must by the grace of God have merited this holy privilege.

When she conceived Christ, she said in that prophetic song which at the present day is the song of all Christianity, as it was yesterday and will be hereafter : " All women, all generations shall call me blessed." The humble Virgin, who had become mother by the Spirit of God, did not guess that all generations would call her by a still fairer

name. Women who listen to me know that there
is no name sweeter, deeper, more full of tenderness
than the name of mother. This name was to be
given in the days to come by all the disciples of
Jesus to Mary, Mother of Jesus. She became,
indeed, our Mother on Calvary, in the profound
mystery of the divine love. Resigned to the
inexorable will of God who condemned her Son
to be crucified, she identified herself with His
sufferings, His woes and His death; and her
anguish, heroically endured, has been the condition of that maternity perpetuated through all the
ages and which the acclamations of the universal
Church have consecrated for ever.

All good and simple souls, all those in whom
the mind has not stifled the heart, all Christians
who have a lively faith, have felt themselves
adopted from that hour by this Blessed creature
in whose heart God placed the well-spring of pity.
By her those choice graces which God pours upon
humanity through mysterious channels, are given
to us.

I may, perhaps, give offence to those who boast
of their reason and their independence, and who
believe it to be unworthy of a man to bow himself
before that Woman who has been so greatly exalted
by God Himself; and, if so, let them be offended.

Let those of simple and sober mind, of large
and sincere heart, hear this : one day when they

can have no more of life, when they feel overwhelming pain which nothing can heal, when, crushed with the thought of their own wretchedness, they dare not look towards God nor call to Him, from the depth of the abysss let them remember that they have a divine Mother, a woman called the Virgin Mary, consecrated on Calvary to be their Mother in the divine order, let them invoke her, and they will be saved.

I know women who, following the spirit of the Virgin Mother to whom they have consecrated themselves, invoke her name ; and, breathing it into the ear of the dying, have gathered up for God hundreds of hardened and desperate sinners.

Oh, repeat this name again, my sisters. You are the chosen instruments to accomplish visibly the invisible task of Mary ; you know how to staunch and heal, and you know also that best balm which soothes and calms all wounds, the balm of affection and kindness. Consequently, when you can murmur the name of the Mother of all Christians in the ear which has need to hear eternal truth, hesitate not to invoke it. You who struggle in darkness and the anguish of evil, seeking in vain for light, for strength and for peace, know that, if you have a Father who watches over you, and a Mediator who loves you, you have also His mother—yours—who will listen to you always, and hold out her sacred hand to bring you back to God and to Christ.

The fourth word which Jesus spake on the Cross is a word of anguish : " My God ! my God ! why hast Thou forsaken me ? "

It is the beginning of a prophetic psalm which paints in letters of fire the unspeakable woes of Jesus crucified.

Indeed, brethren, we cannot imagine or conceive a woe equal to that which overwhelmed the soul of Jesus during the three hours of His crucifixion. He was nailed to the Cross about midday, and He drew His last breath at three o'clock according to the precise statements of the Evangelists.

But I know that many Christians—I have heard them many times—say : " Since Jesus was God, how could He have any sorrow ? God could not suffer, and He who was the Son of God should not suffer ; if He suffered, His pain was drowned in the infinite beatitude of His divinity."

Such a mode of reasoning rests upon the radically false idea that Jesus had humanity only in appearance, that He was not a man in flesh and blood, endowed as we are, and more than we are, with most exquisite sensibility.

Jesus was God indeed, but He was equally man. The human nature and the divine were united in Him without confusion, and each of them preserved their essential properties intact. God has no passions, but man has passions, and the union of the divine with the human nature of Jesus not only did not prevent the sufferings of human nature, but added to them something of the infinite.

Indeed, a nature has a capacity for suffering all the more great as its sensibility is keener and more delicate. Now the union of the divine with the human nature, far from lessening the sensibility, added something of infinity—that is to say, it thereby became an instrument still more perfect for comprehension, for love, for will, for feeling and suffering.

Man cannot be divided : his psychical faculties are closely combined, the attenuation of one is sometimes a detriment and sometimes an advantage to others; thus, a man who is devoid of intellect suffers but little, and you must have remarked the impassibility of certain herculean natures in whom the muscles are everything. On the contrary, you may have observed the particular, refined, and subtle sensibility of intellectual beings; a mere word can wound them, because, from their keener intelligence, they understand better and feel more profoundly. Now Jesus having the most delicate, the most refined, the most intelligent, and the most loving human nature, must, since His physical nature was admirably adapted to His human intellect and moral nature, have endured unutterable agony ; and we may say that

He climbed to the last step of the degrees of the ladder of pain.

Let us consider Him only on the Cross. It is written in the sacred book of His people that He must be crucified, and He himself announced it; He said : " I have to be baptised with the Baptism of Blood, and how am I straitened until it be accomplished." He said also: " I am come to cast fire on the earth, and what will I but that it be kindled." And this fire consumed Him first of all.

Crucifixion is the most frightful suffering which has ever been invented by human cruelty. And what is wonderful is, that the Jews did not crucify, and that Jesus who belonged to the Jewish nation was crucified, and that at the demand of His own people. The Romans did not crucify their own citizens, they slew with the sword—a nobler death. But if the Roman citizens died by the sword, the inhabitants of conquered provinces were crucified like slaves, an ignominious death, reserved for the most despised class of men. The suffering was atrocious, because the death was slow and left all his faculties to the sufferer, who witnessed his own ignominious death, exposed naked before the whole multitude, the whole nation.

The punishment took place in the light of day, and whoever passed along the road by the side of which the cross was raised might see, insult, or pity the victim.   And in addition to this frightful martyrdom was the devouring thirst and the horrible fever which consumed the crucified. Jesus knew this pain.   He knew another also, the pain which came from the people who surrounded Him.   At such a moment, amid the wild crowd there prevailed a sort of contagion of insult; each one tried who could blaspheme the most, they recalled the words which had been pronounced by Jesus and made of them a weapon against Him; because He had said: "I am able to destroy the Temple and after three days to rebuild it," it was urged against Him as a blasphemy worthy of death.   They ironically reproached Him also for His divine Sonship: "If Thou be the Son of God, come down from the Cross."   It was in the midst of the agony of His punishment that they addressed to Him those reproaches.   When He said He was the Son of God, they would not listen to Him, and His word had no power; now that He was nailed on the Cross they said: "Answer, and let God save Thee, if He will, since Thou art the Son of God."

A cowardly insult!

A clever man once said to me: "If Jesus were the Son of God, He ought at that moment to have caused the nails to fall from His cross, and, springing among the crowd, to have cried: Here is the Son of God!"

This is to understand divine things but little!

It is not by a sudden enlightenment but by the gentleness of persuasion that God will open hearts to Him.

Such were the insults and wrongs to which Jesus had to submit when He uttered that cry of anguish in a dialect which certain Romans could not understand: "Eli! Eli!" which means, "My God! my God!" Those who did not understand Him said: "This man calleth Elias!" and they joked with that unconscious cruelty which is one of the worst traits of humanity, and which takes possession of crowds when they flock in their curiosity to behold a bloody death.

This pain He knew. All His doctrine, all the good that He did, all His power is therein. His Father did not come down to save Him; the hour had come in which He gave His Son, a defence-less victim. His friends were there, His mother, John, the holy women, and all of no avail. His mother experienced an anguish which pierced her with seven swords, His friends could do nothing, and their powerlessness was for them a torture the more. There were there priests and high priests and all that was most respectable in the land, but these insulted Him pitilessly, with the irony which belongs to superior people.

Yet there was something still more terrible,

more atrociously cruel in the abyss of evils wherein
Jesus was cast by the will of His Father.

Our members may be tortured as were those of
the martyrs given over to the beasts, or to man
more cruel than the beasts; we may be devoured
by the fever of death, our hearts reduced to a
stone, calcined by the flame of sorrow; we may
be the mark for every insult, whether on the part
of the careless and brutal populace or of the
educated, more refined in their cruelty; we may
be victims of the vengeance of political power or
of the anathemas of religious power; we may see
our friends helpless witnesses of our torture, increasing our grief a hundredfold by their anguish;
but in this lamentable state one last refuge is
open to us, against the violence of the hatred of
men: conscience, and in the conscience, God—
God who sees justice and loves it; God who sees
sacrifice and blesses it, who recognises devotion,
who beholds our anguish and assuages it.

But Jesus, at the hour when He cried: "My
God, my God, why hast Thou forsaken me?"
Jesus who had divinity in Himself, in His intellect, in His will, Jesus at one moment repulsed by
His Father who treated Him as the victim laden
with all the sins of the world, had not any longer
this consoling sense of the divinity living in Him;
he lost it—and it is frightful to say so, though no
heresy—it is frightful, I say, but it is the truth;

hence that terrible cry so full of agony which came from His heart and fell from the Cross as the last word of human suffering: "My God, my God! why hast Thou forsaken me?"

We have a foretaste of this bitter suffering when at certain hours our spirit troubles our will, we feel God no longer in the deep of our conscience. We have a foretaste of that terrible moment which Jesus knew and which can only be compared to the damnation of souls for ever plunged in that darkness wherein the will of God does not shine, and frozen in that icy cold where divine love penetrates no longer. Not that His human and His divine natures were disunited, they were inseparable, but the humanity of Jesus no longer felt, as we can feel, that God was in Him.

And now, in face of the Crucified, I have the right to say: You who weep, complain no more; be angry no more; you who are dying, look at Him and send towards God the same cry which He uttered; see if there be a sorrow like unto His sorrow! What we can see of God is a ray; what we can feel of God is a drop of ambrosia, while that which Jesus looked upon was the sun, and what He felt was an immense flood encompassing heaven and earth. Conceive, then, what He experienced when the flood, like an intercepted source, no longer intoxicated Him with its infinite sweetness.

I have said that one of the great agonies of the crucified was the agony of thirst, and this Jesus endured.   A moment after He felt His dereliction by God His Father, He cried : " I thirst."

One of the Evangelists who witnessed this scene tells us it and interprets the word of Jesus. In order to emphasise the fact that the events in the life and the death of the Saviour had been foretold by prophecy he makes this comment :

" Jesus having accomplished all things, that the Scripture might be fulfilled, said : I thirst."

This prophetic word of Scripture was that Jesus on His cross should be given vinegar to drink. The Romans prepared two sorts of beverage for those condemned to be crucified.   The first was a mixture of incense, myrrh and wine, a stupefying liquor which, lulling the senses of the patient, calmed the last hours of agony.

When you read the account of the Passion, I beg you to remark that this beverage was presented to Jesus at the moment of His elevation on the Cross; but He refused it, choosing to endure His suffering in the full clearness of His human spirit, and to taste the chalice of His sorrows to the dregs without diminution of its bitterness.

The second beverage, destined for the soldiers and for the condemned when they were about to die, and with which they were wont to moisten their dry and burning lips, was vinegar or a sort of sour wine. When Jesus said : "I thirst," they presented to His lips a wet sponge ; and then the last word which the Scripture had said about Him, that vinegar should be presented to Him, was accomplished.

This thirst of Jesus has a deeper sense. When He uttered the cry: "*Sitio !*" He not only expressed the horrible sufferings of the Crucified but He expressed also the inner thirst of His soul, His burning desires, His ardent love, and this thirst was more vehement and more devouring still than the other.

Jesus then wished and His love thirsted with so much ardour on the Cross for you, my brethren, for us, for all humanity ; He desired to communicate to you, to us, to all, the divine life which He had in its fulness.

Have you an idea of the devouring thirst and ardour of desire which takes hold of the soul in which faith is living as a burning fire ? It is difficult to understand it in this languid age in which it seems the height of wisdom to extinguish all desire—in this time wherein scepticism has weakened so many minds, and the vehemence of earthly appetites has extinguished higher aspirations, in which we must seek in vain for those noble and undaunted natures to whom nothing is impossible. The thirst of good, honest, and

N

virtuous hearts inflamed with the desire to extend
their wisdom and to bring in the reign of justice
and of truth, consumes no longer our worn-out
natures.   We may well speak of being worn out
before Him who came to give us the intensity of
the divine life, and if we are men who do not
understand the holy foolishness of truth, the holy
eagerness for justice and progress ; if we call ourselves conservatives—as if the word to conserve was
one of the Gospel and not rather a negation of the
Gospel—if we call ourselves conservatives instead
of progressives, insatiable of life, it is because, in
truth, faith consumes us no longer.

Leave conservatism to God, because He is the
infinite, but we whose truth is relative, whose
justice is limited, we who always are in movement,
ought always to advance.

You will say that we have a revelation.   But
revelation is ever growing, in its effects, in its
applications, in that species of fever which it
communicates to humanity.   Of what then will
you be "conservative"—of your imperfections, your
limits, your wretchedness ?   That is to betray God
who created you to advance for ever, and, if you
withdraw yourselves from His divine impulse, God
will raise up the thirsty and unsatisfied to perpetuate in humanity that which ought to grow
and will grow, that thirst which the Crucified
experienced in His passion and of which He

uttered a cry piercing and immortal in the face of heaven and earth.

In this, as in all things, He is our model; though we overthrow the framework in which you have established your tranquil and selfish life, though we inspire you with the conviction that that which is to-day will not be to-morrow, that your tent is pitched but for a while, that you must strike it to bear it elsewhere; yet as disciples of Him who was athirst for all good, for all justice and all perfection, we would utter with Him and after Him that piercing and terrible cry: "*Sitio !*"

That which sprang from the lips of the Crucified is never silent; the cry uttered on Calvary has entered into the very heart of humanity, so as to move, and, if need be, to melt, it, for it is an irresistible force, a devouring flame.

Blessed be Thou, O Jesus, Thy words do their work in spite of all, for they are spirit and life, and nothing can repress spirit and life.

At the hour when Jesus pronounced this word nothing that He desired existed, and all that existed was against Him; the multitude angry and disappointed, His disciples terrified and scattered; the Jewish authorities triumphant, convinced that they had made an end of this dangerous man, a disturber, a seducer, a blas-

phemer and revolutionary ; they were happy and
satisfied, persuaded that the drama of Calvary
would have no morrow, and that He who hung
there thirsting in His agony would die of His
thirst. Far from dying, He has conquered, and we
live by His thirst, for it has excited in us the holy
fever of progress, the irresistible effect of Him
who, dying upon His Cross, has given us the power
to dream, to desire, and to be ambitious of all.

O Christ ! Thou wert athirst at that hour !
since then it is we who quench Thy thirst.
Every time that a soul comes to Thee it is like
the cup of fresh water given by the Samaritan to
the tired traveller. For the Crucified whose
tongue clave to the roof of His mouth, every man
who is converted, every people and nation converted, are as streams of living water.

Ah, if in this city there were to be a universal
rallying to the Crucified, and if from the crowd
there came out this great cry : "*Sitio !*" would you
be disquieted and affrighted ? There is but one
thing which affrights, and that is man when he is
far from God ; but if he be in revolt against God, I
know well that you are right to be afraid, because
he is of all beings the most terrible. Do you
desire never to fear any more the tumultuous
movement of human society ? Come near the
Crucified and quench His thirst in giving yourself
to Him. Calvary has never been a cause of fear

for any soul, for any people. It has always been
a place of reconciliation ; for the Cross is the Tree
of Peace, under the shadow of which all men must
find themselves sooner or later if they would meet
each other as brethen.

The sixth word of Jesus is this : " *Consummatum
est :* it is finished ! "

This word should be the law of life. When a
life is finished we should be able to say, not in a
vain and formal sense, but in all the fulness of the
meaning : It is finished.

Now, my brethen. for what was it that Jesus
came into this world ? He often told us that
it was to accomplish the work which His
heavenly Father had given Him to do—the work
of salvation indicated by His name of Saviour ;
He came to teach truth to men, to give them an
example of virtue, to communicate to them eternal
life and the Spirit of God.

Now to accomplish that work He needed to
bear witness to the truth, to present the model of
an absolutely holy life, and to enter by the means
at the disposal of God alone into the conscience
of men, to inoculate them with the Spirit of
God.

In this manner, Jesus was truly the Saviour of
humanity. For that which kills humanity is the
ignorance of truth ; it is vice and all the evils
which it engenders ; it is the privation of the

divine Spirit, or the power by the aid of which we can strive against the evils and the vices which devour us, and against the darkness which overwhelms our spirit.

Therefore Jesus was—He often said so—the witness to truth, the example given to all those who would follow the good. Therefore He called Himself the living fountain which slakes thirst, the source of the spirit which overflows the world and brings to it eternal life.

Therefore, when on the Cross Jesus said this great word: " It is finished!" this was to say: I have borne witness to the truth, I have shown you the way, I have opened to you the source of the Spirit of God which I have in fulness.

And He did this by sorrow.

Sorrow is a great teacher; we can do nothing, even Jesus Christ Himself could do nothing, without sorrow. Without it a work alway wants the final seal. The poet who has never suffered can never draw from his lyre the most moving and sublime sounds ; the scientific man who has never suffered in order to conquer Nature and force the gates behind which her mysteries are hidden, will find Nature rebellious and her gates sealed. The philosopher who has not suffered, who has but constructed a system from his poor ideas, who talks of pessimism after having lived a joyous and tranquil life—of idealism after having lived,

like other men, in the brutal realities of sense,
who talks of positivism after having gaily
suppressed all higher forces, whose mysterious
action uplifts all men of action—conquerors, rulers
of the people, founders of races and of religions—
such beings, whoever they are, if sorrow has not
touched them, remain ineffectual; they want the
power of persuasion and ascendency, they lack
dignity and majesty.

Whoever would bear witness to truth must
suffer, and, if need be, die for truth. Whoever
would give an example must give it in trial and
even unto death; whoever aspires to open a new
path unto men, must be ready to place not his
statue but his dead body at the entrance of the
path to which he leads them.

Statues are rife in decaying civilisations; but
they often need to be taken away, for they
encumber the road, and in their place a man must
leave his tomb, more eloquent than a vain effigy.

I admire the wisdom of the Orientals. At
Constantinople you may see the mausoleums
of the great Caliphs at the cross-roads. These
funereal and magnificent monuments declare to
the people that the dead man who is laid under
the marble, granite or porphyry, has not left
his people, but still serves unseen the cause for
which he laid down his life.

I know not if the custom is contrary to the

principles of hygiene, but I know well that it has a great moral effect.

A man of our day is only truly worthy of honour on condition that he bears on his brow the glory of suffering and martyrdom. Sorrow and blood consecrate everything.

From this point of view no one ever reached the level of Jesus who died on the Cross, for He alone can say : It is finished, because He sanctioned by His death—and by the most terrible death—the testimony which He rendered to truth and the examples which He gave to men by a life of incomparable sanctity.

He has done more and better; He consecrated by His death the full right of humanity to enter into the Spirit of God.

The Spirit of God—I hold to that word of the Gospel—is closed to us if Jesus has not opened its source.

I spoke just now of the body which I like to see on the roads to mark to us the higher point to which we must go. The Cross of Jesus planted on the road of humanity is the living source from which we must draw, if we would have the life which never dies. And we are now free to enter on this bloody road.

You will ask why the way was previously closed, and I answer because the inexorable justice of God placed a barrier before us.

Earth and human reason are not everything. Above the forces of earth and of reason you must not forget the divine force. You cannot explain why, before Jesus, humanity crouched under an iron sky. All the gods which humanity made to itself wielded the thunderbolt, and all societies which modelled themselves on the image of those gods were societies wherein violence and slavery bore sway. Because they knew not those divine forces which are ours, and they were crushed beneath the heavy weight of human justice.

And after Jesus came the complete change created by His sacrifice and His cross. There appeared in heaven a divine phenomenon, the reconciliation and the re-establishment of eternal order and eternal justice. Therefore when Jesus said: " *Consummatum est,*" it is as though He had said: The reign of human slavery, the reign of a terrible God and of His overpowering and inflexible justice which spared nothing, all that partook of the nature of the world given up to evil and the wrath of God, is finished. I bring it to an end.

He brought it to an end, in fact, by His sorrow and His sacrifice.

Man has only one means of conquering evil and conciliating justice, and that is to accept everything as the necessary chastisement and expiation of moral evil. Jesus accepted infinite suffering; He is the Lamb of God that takes away the sins of the world. Thanks to Him, Heaven and man have been reconciled—the face of God, to speak in human language, is softened and smiling; the angry master has become the heavenly Father. The Father indeed rules the modern world, and therefore in the Victim of Calvary I worship the Creator of the great human brotherhood, for the human brotherhood is only the social consequence of the divine brotherhood. You who speak of human fatherhood and who deny your Father in heaven, are confuted by the most terrible facts, and you see your brethren strive the one against the other in oppression and in blood, with implacable fury.

But when you would cause to reign upon earth that holy brotherhood which goes so far as to surrender in charity all its own rights for those who have nothing, the holy brotherhood which staunches the wounds of poor wretches dying on all sides of us; which draws near without fear to men whose mouth is full of blasphemy and whose hands are blackened by work; the holy brotherhood which forgets itself to enclose in a warm and universal embrace all the members of the human family, you must remember that that brotherhood can only come through the heavenly Father, the God of the Gospel.

Your science, your philosophy, your social and

political economy will never succeed in bringing it about. Whenever you forget the great Crucified Saviour you will fall back under the yoke of the laws of the old humanity before its redemption. Your lips will call men brethren, but in reality you will find before you enemies alone; the enemy will be he who has less than you, who does not think with you, who will take your place; while the friend, the true brother, is he who follows the example of Jesus in saying: " Love your enemies." The friend is he who lives in dependence on the heavenly Father and who says to you: Since we call God our Father, we are sprung from Him and return to Him, why then should we dispute about this atom of earth which we shall leave to-morrow? It is not worth the trouble of strife and contentions, it ought only to be for us a point in which we meet, a point of ephemeral union which we must quit to gain a higher and a better one in the eternal country whose supreme law is the union of all in infinite truth, good, and love.

The last word of Jesus: " Father, into Thy hands I commend my spirit," is the formula of death. After having spoken it, He uttered a great cry and bowed His head and died.

There are three ways of living, and so there are three ways of dying. Some live in animalism, some in humanity, others in God. Those who live in animalism, borrow more or less from the instincts which constitute and characterise it, and they will end as animals; those who live in a human fashion, in a more or less elevated manner at the pleasure of their capricious reason, of their selfish and fickle will, and of their small ambitions, will also end, in a manner more or less distinguished, in humanity. Lastly, there are those who, masters of their instincts and of themselves, live in God and they will end in God.

Jesus lived entirely in God, His Father; that which was material in Him and belonged to the life of instinct was absolutely subordinate to human reason and will, as His human reason and will were absolutely subordinate to the wisdom and the will of His Father.

You therefore see the sublime and divine sense of that word which ended the mortal life of Jesus: " Father, into Thy hands I commend my spirit!" In thus giving His soul into His Father's hands, He gave Him everything. You will remark that Jesus ended as a free man, He was not conquered by death, though He allowed death to finish its work in Him.

According to the story of the Evangelists, Jesus on the Cross held up His head; He spake the words which I have made my poor comments upon with His eyes fixed on heaven, and after having pronounced the last He gave a great cry, then bowed His head and rendered up His spirit. That was the end.

But what is important for us to see here is that we are destined to inevitable, fatal, necessary death; and in virtue of the very laws of our constitution, we have to choose between three kinds of death.

Alas! it is the fate of a great number of men to die in an animal fashion. Hardly freed from instinct they obey the law of instinct up to the last hour, they give to the earth that which belongs to it, or rather, earth takes them again; sprung from the dust, they move for a moment above the dust to which they return as the animals return, without consciousness.

To die as a man is to bring to death some intellect, some will, some conscience; the majority allow themselves to be surprised by the end which comes upon them unexpectedly, because they turn their eyes from it. And to see men so careless might make us believe that not to think of death was to avoid it. Pagans were braver, they looked at it as it came. Want of energy, enervation of will, attachment to present life, the unbelief of civilisation, has increased among us the terror of death. Therefore the final word of tenderness in our homes is to veil the imminence of death and the approach of the terrible abyss from the eyes of those we love.

Some, however, have a consciousness of their end, but most of them die without repentance, leaving regretfully a life whose mysterious morrow fills them with terror.

Unbelievers hope to leave behind them certain works by which they will survive in humanity. Round the coffin which contains their remains, their friends will come to hold converse with them ; they declare that they know, and they teach, that there is nothing left of them, and that they talk not only to a dead man, but to one who has no existence, yet they will talk to him all the same and call upon him : " Thy memory will endure in humanity which thou hast served : thou wilt be an example for all those who survive thee ; thy son, thy wife, thy friends will follow thy precepts, &c. &c."

Such is the rite of human funerals. I am willing to admit that certain traces remain in humanity to witness to the passage of those who have lived in it. No doubt, a man of science, a writer, a poet, a politician, a conqueror, do not entirely die out of that humanity which they have taught, enchanted, attracted, and perhaps terrified.

But humanity does not contain the life of the soul, and the earth does not contain the life of eternity. I do not know what certain people think of it, that is their affair, but they cannot deny that there are among men many natures greedy of eternity, who are straitened in this vast earth, in this vast universe, as much as in the ditch into which their dead body is thrown; and how will they end, what will they do with their soul in the face of death? To whom will they commend their spirits?

Jesus has taught us the true way to die; death, which will come for those whom we love and for ourselves, truly the death which we must look in the face, the death which is the condition of our entrance into the world towards which we tend, that death, I hope, for you, will be such as Jesus has taught.

When you come to that hour—I speak not only to the dying, but also to those who stand about the dying, I say to all, help them to die as Jesus died. Try to awaken in the conscience of him who is about to go the idea of the heavenly Father, who has given us a task to fulfil here below, and who will judge us.

The awakening conscience will understand in the clearness of death, what good it has done and what evil; it will render thanks to God and ask pardon of Him, and these two acts sum up the whole; the life which they end is pure, and the death which they prepare is worthy of God. And then you may sleep in peace. What good you have done will remain, for good is like God, imperishable, eternal. Your domestic virtues will be the flame of the hearth which is desolated by death, and this contagious flame will light up others—you will have sons and daughters who will perpetuate your virtues. The good which you have done may perhaps be ignored by men, but that matters nothing ; you may look to heaven, for the sake of which you have sought for truth, for perfection, and for the source of all things, and you may say to your heavenly Father : " Into Thy hands I commend my life, my soul, my very being, O Thou whom Christ has taught me to love ! "

That is the true way to die.

Jesus has thus left us all knowledge and all examples ; the knowledge of life and the power of living, the knowledge of death and the power of dying in God.

Men scorn the knowledge of how to die. We, however, esteem it, for I declare that those alone know how to die well who have been the boldest in life. Those who have had in life the boldness of spirit and the help of that Father whose sons they know themselves to be, go to their death as Jesus went.

We know not how we shall die ; perhaps from a bullet which seeks us out in defending our country, perhaps at the bedside of another, carried off by contagion. We know not whether we shall die in want, abandoned by all our friends and overwhelmed with insult, as was Jesus.

The greatest sometimes end thus, and we must look for all possibilities. Who can tell whether we shall die at the hand of a murderer or in some explosion?

We live on an earth where everything may assail us. We should be ready to render up our soul after we have lived valiantly. Suppose you have but a second to look death in the face; then remember the Calvary of the dying Jesus, and have but one word with which to quit this world; but let it spring from the depths of your conscience: "Father, into Thy hands I commend my spirit!"

And so ending, you will leave to those who stand around the joy of children who go towards their father, those who go to God.

Those who go to God are a great means of union. You will leave behind you a track of light and a track of virtues; you will have the glory of dying as Jesus died, not, indeed, in saving the world—that only belongs to God—but in saving some of those beings who are dear to you in the world; and that is the highest glory of the children of God.

VIII

THE PRACTICAL MEANS FOR BELIEVING IN THE DIVINITY OF JESUS CHRIST

In placing before you the difficulties of the belief in the divinity of Jesus Christ—difficulties inherent partly in the very act of faith, partly in our own nature, partly in the circumstances of our lives—I fear that I may have kept you in suspense and perhaps discouraged you.

To see obstacles before us always slackens our impulse and paralyses action, except in those valiant and strongly tempered natures whom difficulty stimulates and peril emboldens.

But in speaking to you as I have done I had an after-thought of pity. I said to myself, we must feel for those who do not believe ; and to show that they are worthy of our pity, we must admit what is, in fact, the reality—that there are difficulties in believing. Then, counting also on the generous substratum of human nature, I thought those who know where the difficulty lies in believing will know best how to conquer it.

And now a practical question arises which has, no doubt, occurred to you. Do the means of believing exist? If so, what are they? Does it depend upon our own will and our own energy?

I cannot terminate this series of lectures on the faith in the divinity of Jesus Christ without showing you that there do exist means for believing in this divinity—practical means, which are in your own hands, and which it only depends upon you to employ.

As science and philosophy, morals and education, art and politics have their proper methods and processes, so faith has its own. I will go farther, and say that the processes of science and philosophy, morals and education, the methods of art and politics are not within the power of everybody. Not everybody can aspire to be a man of science, a philosopher, a moralist, a teacher, an artist of renown, or a leader of nations; while the processes and means of belief belong to all, for all the world can and ought to aspire to belief.

Between the Gospel and human things there is always this difference—to the honour of the Gospel—that human things are the affair of a chosen few—and I say this of even universal suffrage, however universal it be—while the things of the Gospel belong to all. I will show you, in fact, that it is in the power of all to believe in the divinity of Jesus if only they have a sincere mind and an upright will.

When I speak of the means of believing in the divinity of Jesus, notice that I do not exclude that divine, invisible, sacred influence which surrounds man and all creatures, and which, when this action is a divine and supernatural succour of humanity, we call, in theological language, Grace. This divine action is everywhere, but it is especially there, and it makes its power felt even unconsciously to those who experience it.

Notice, moreover, that I am not now addressing myself to those tranquil believers whom I have already compared to infants asleep on the bosom of their mother, to those believers for whom faith is a pious heritage, who having been born on their knees before Jesus Christ, Son of God, live on their knees before Him, the Lord whom they have always worshipped, and who die embracing the Cross which has saved them.

Therefore I except all children, many women, many Christians, and I consider only those natures who find themselves to-day more or less troubled in their faith—the hesitating, the indifferent, those who claim the right to reflect, to argue, those who wish to be a law unto themselves, disposing of their own powers and of their life as a master disposes of his property.

I speak to you, then, for I know you well;

because it is not possible to have lived more than half a century and have found oneself face to face in the great struggle of life with difficulties which beat against the fortress of the faith in all intelligent and free consciences ; it is not possible, I say, to have lived thus without taking account of how terrible it is to maintain a position unvanquished wherein all would be overthrown and ruined if it did not rest upon foundations which man cannot destroy.

And again I exclude not only children and those who have the simple faith of the labourer, I exclude men of corrupt will, those who have chosen their place ; I exclude stupid incredulity, self-satisfied unbelief, the proud and vain spirit which measures and weighs us, finds us wanting, and scorns us from above.

I must exclude him, if he will have it so ; but if he will remain and listen, I will yet accept him in the profound respect which I always have, even for those who attack, I do not say the priest but his faith.

Well, the field once marked out, the question which I have laid down returns : Are there means of belief, what is their nature, are they in our power ?

The means of belief exist, since it is a duty to believe. We cannot admit for a moment that we are bound by an obligation which it is impossible to fulfil; whoever aspires to belief in Jesus Christ with a faith which rests on reason and on motives such as minds demand when culture has ripened them for independence and liberty, must in the first place put himself in personal relations with Jesus Christ as a real and historic personage. Jesus Christ, the Son of Man, declared and taught His divine Sonship. I ask you who wish to believe, who feel the need of it, and who often say : I would and I cannot; I ask you to put yourselves in a personal and direct relation with Him who has affirmed, taught, and proclaimed these prodigious and unheard-of things.

We are, you say, in relation with Him; but that is an illusion. You are not yet there—you do not know Jesus—I do not say the Jesus of dogma, the Jesus of the creed, whose sublime formula is, for the faithful, merely a summary of all that He is in reality—you do not know the Jesus of history, living, acting, preaching, teaching, suffering, persecuted, founding His work and doctrine on His death and sacrifice. You do not know the Jesus of the Gospels as His disciples picture Him in the sincerity of their soul and the fidelity of their recollection, so that the ages might always guard His ineffaceable and incorruptible image.

In saying this I do not wish to reproach men of letters too vehemently, although I certainly have the right to do so, for many times in my life as a priest I have met cultivated men steeped in the literature of their time, knowing all the religious and irreligious books which have recently appeared in France, Germany or elsewhere, able to sum them up and to analyse them, but ignorant of the Gospel. They had never read it through as a whole, they have heard it read in some degree in their childhood, perhaps in later life a few fragments when they have been in the holidays to the little church of their village, and that is all !

Now, how can you be in direct and personal relations with a man, a man who belongs to history, if you do not know his life? Nor can you know the life of Jesus if you do not seek its elements in the Gospel.

I have heard many men say : I read the Gospel, but I do not understand it. Difficulties arise on each page, and I cannot get on with my reading.

Allow me to answer to this objection, that there are three ways of reading a book : with the critical spirit, with imagination more or less dreamy and sentimental, and with the conscience.

When one reads with the spirit of criticism, it is to judge ; with imagination it is as a distraction ; with conscience it is to become better.

Read the Gospel, not with your critical spirit, nor with your poet's imagination, but with your conscience ; later, you who reason may pass to criticism; and you poets, to imagination and to all that you can conceive of what is beautiful.

But in the name of that Book which has no equal, in the name of the divine nobleness and wisdom which breathes in each of its words, I ask you to read it in the first place with your simple reason and with your conscience. Read in this spirit it will make your conscience thrill at every page before the good, the true and the beautiful which transfigure them, and you will often close the book, moved and delighted, to say with Rousseau: "If the life and death of Socrates are those of a wise man, the life and death of Jesus were those of a God."

You will notice that in asking you to read the Gospels with your conscience I have no other end than to bring about by that reading your placing your conscience in relation with the hero of that book, Jesus Christ.

I do not like to bring myself forward, it is always a delicate thing, but I do it now for your instruction. The study of history and constant reading of the Gospel have allowed me to bring myself in contact with Christ; I have called upon Him as one can call upon one who has long since passed away from earth, but who yet remains engraved ineffaceably on the pages where every candid mind can find Him, and I bear you witness that I saw arise before me a human being whom

none can resist; He has inspired me with
absolute confidence; a confidence which will lead
me, following Him, through fire and water; His
moral beauty is dazzling, and His whole teaching
instinct with the highest truth. His holiest
shines forth in the least of His actions, a virtue
goes out from Him, He exercises a magic from
which no sincere and simple heart can escape.

Whatever be the result of this reading, I ask
you to read. I do not bring forward proofs,
I would give you the blessing of faith by healing
you of the evil of incredulity. It is my duty and
my right. You ask me how you shall believe, I
point out the means as I know them, simply and
as experience has taught me to know them.

Before all things take the eternal Gospel as a
book for your bedside and as your travelling
book. When you are tired of the business of the
day, or the fatigues of life, read and re-read it,
not as a poet, not as a critical scholar, nor as a
learned professor, not as an interpreter or a
historian: read it as a man. There is something
grander than imagination, than science, than mind
or genius—were it the mind of the whole world
and the greatest genius—there is something
which I put above all; and you will agree with
me; this something, with which you must read the
Gospel, is conscience.

Genius can only attain to phenomena and their

causes. Conscience penetrates to the good, and good is the last word of the supreme cause, of God and Jesus Christ.

When you have read and re-read the Gospel under these conditions, you will be in relation with Jesus ; you will observe that I do not know what will happen afterwards, but you will be in relation with the human being whom I have indicated to you as declaring in a solemn manner His own divinity. Does He deserve belief or not ? That is the sovereign question, and it can only be solved by those who have placed themselves in close and lasting union with Christ.

The intimate commerce of the conscience with the person of Jesus by constant and attentive reading of the Gospel is the first step of him who is seeking faith ; but it is not sufficient.

Many, indeed, among the contemporaries of Jesus found themselves in contact with Him, heard Him preach, saw Him cure the sick, and yet, what a difference ! Some believed in Him and became His disciples. Others remained indifferent, withdrew themselves from Him, and even became his adversaries.

Whence, then, comes this variety of attitude ? Why are some enlightened and others blinded ? What passes in the secret recesses of the soul at the moment when Christ is evoked either by the reading of the Gospel or by the living word of the apostle ?

We cannot tell. When the light remains sterile and is not changed into faith and virtue, it is not that light is wanting to man, but that man betrays light.

Jesus will teach us why and wherefore, and will deliver to us the true secret of belief.

" If any man will come after me," He often said to His disciples and to the crowd, " let him deny himself, take up his cross and follow me."

To come after Jesus is to believe, to come after Him is to enter into the faith of His divinity.

There can be no doubt on this point. The disciple of Jesus, the man who would follow Him, must believe what his Master declares of Himself, and, consequently, His divine Sonship. But in order to arrive at this faith, Jesus teaches as a necessary condition the renouncement of our own personality, the sacrifice symbolised in carrying the Cross.

The way is strait. If you believe that it is easy to be a Christian, disabuse yourself of the notion. Certainly the gate which leads to the Kingdom is strait, and we are thankful for it. Jesus will not have in His following the common herd—the selfish, the satisfied, those who are incapable of devotion, of forgetfulness of self and of sacrifice ; He rejects them, and He teaches in unmistakable terms : " If a man will come after me, let him deny himself."

We have to find what personal abnegation and sacrifice of self and one's own individuality are.

Human personality may find fault with itself in spirit, reason, will, ambitions, interests and private affections : but above private reason and minds narrowed by systems there is that reason to which I continually appeal, impersonal, eternal reason ; above the will governed by our own private interests and aspirations there is the universal will of God and of good ; above light, selfish and passing affections there is disinterested and eternal love which never passes away.

When Jesus demands the sacrifice and renunciation of self, He does not demand the sacrifice of eternal reason or universal will, of good and all the higher interests of humanity and of God. He demands the sacrifice of our own ideas, our mean ambitions, our selfish interests, all that constitutes in the human sense of the word our personality ; but it must be added that to this personality man clings more than anything else.

He disdains universal, incorruptible reason. He does not even think of universal and general good ; interest, unless it touches him directly, that of his country, and still more, that of humanity in regard to which disclaimers make such a noise— these interests hold but little place in his individual life.

A complex and greedy selfishness fills the heart

and tyrannises over the mind of man ; selfishness of the mind, in our petty systems ; selfishness of love in our little affections ; selfishness of personal interests, for which all dispute, and which are not worth the struggle.

Now, if you would follow Jesus, all this must be sacrificed. He has declared it : sacrifice is the door by which we come to Him :

"If any one will come after me, let him renounce himself."

It is a hard thing to ask. The more self in the human sense is considerable in our little world, the more are we set upon our own philosophy and systematic science, puffed up with power, dominating other men by mental influence, authority or money ; the more we are engaged in multiple and ardent affections, the less we are ready to believe.

I can give you an historical proof of this. The Gospel which I have invited you to study, the Gospel which contains the living, wonderful, irresistible Jesus, tells how He appeared before His nation.

There were men in power—there always are ; bread may be wanting, but power, religious and national power, are never wanting.

There were men of science, doctors of the law, who knew that law down to the last iota, and who boasted of it as their supreme title of glory.

There were—there always are—the rich, even

when others are dying of hunger. They maltreated their servants and sent them out in ambush to rob families who were their enemies or to seize the property of the poor. Happy in their lives—they are always so—having all on their side, they grew fat like the Epicureans, having no remorse because they did not believe in the supreme Judge, exhausting all that life can give, closing their hearts to all pity.

And then there were poor people, without knowledge, without riches, without power,

I have forgotten one category; that of the "holy people," who said: We are perfect; we observe the law, we wash our hands before and after meals; we carry large phylacteries according to tradition; we fast rigorously twice in the week; we cover our heads with ashes; those were the good, the eternal Pharisees.

Well, Jesus came. Power rejected Him, the rich families disdained Him, the learned men and doctors of the law repulsed Him as a blasphemer of the law; the "holy people" were the most inexorable towards Him, the Pharisees pursued Him with their hate as an impious person.

But the poor Galileans—the most despised in all Jerusalem, the people who did not much keep the law, who recognised that they were even a little unfaithful to it; who did not pretend to know the teaching of the sacred Books—

those Galileans, unlettered men, without power, without fortune, without legal sanctity ; those Galileans, Peter, Paul, John, James, Bartholomew, Matthew, a publican—all belonged to that little circle which recognised Jesus.   Just because they had practised the abnegation of self, they felt that their individuality was so poor that they could without difficulty put it on one side.

You will see, the obstacle is always the same.

We, who transmit to the world in the sincerity of our faith the words of Jesus, have assuredly no other pretension than to be an echo of the eternal Word which moved and enlightened the earth. Yet we speak to an organised world, to men who have power and talent—and talent is the great power of our day—or who have fortune and the influence which riches give.   We speak even to " holy people," and where does the Word of Jesus find an echo ?

Power is often suspicious of it ; men who govern opinion by science and by philosophy, of which they seem to have the monopoly, disdain it as a worn-out word ; they would willingly reject it as rubbish abandoned to the scavenger.

Nor can men who are satisfied in their wealth hear the echo of eternity.   They are not interested in it, they care only for the stir and whirl of affairs.

When you see these things reproduced in their

living reality, always in virtue of an unerring law,
remember this : that if you would believe in Jesus
you must renounce the self which is the obstacle ;
without which you will remain in yourself, never
attaining to Him who calls you and who has laid
down as a condition of the power to reach Him,
abnegation of self and of the complex selfishness
which is its essence.

I hear you say : The door is too strait, and the
road too steep.

I admit it, and to attain to Jesus strenuous
men are wanted; as He said, the kingdom of
heaven is not a kingdom of the weak, it is a
kingdom of the strong. The violent take it by
force.

If man were limited to his own energies and
given over to his own aspirations, he would never
arrive at faith ; in order to believe, a divine force,
a secret, irresistible and gentle action of the
Spirit is needed ; aided by grace, man can rise
above himself, and, above all, can place himself in
contact with the transcending reality of God.

There is in the Gospel a profound saying on
this subject, which has often arrested me, and in
the mystery of which I have often loved to lose
my thoughts. Jesus says : " No man can come to
me unless my Father draw him."

I have asked myself how God draws us. I
have interrogated my conscience, the foundation

of our being which men cannot change, nor human surroundings alter—for there, thanks be to God, we have to do with eternity only. I look at this principle which aspires to unlimited truth, to untrammelled good, to absolute beauty, to ideal perfection, and I have felt this and I have said to myself: It is the movement of the Father who draws to Him every intelligent creature, and, by that very fact, to Jesus, the realisation under a human form of the ideal of God.

Philosophers, with your vain systems, politicians, with your ephemeral legislations, men of letters, with your fantasies, you cannot sound this secret and unfathomable gulf—you cannot influence these movements of the infinite and the eternal.

In spite of all the influences which can alter him superficially, man is drawn by the Father. And I say : If the Father draws us towards the beautiful, the good, total perfection, and the cloudless absolute, then He will lead us to Jesus, Son of God.

For Jesus, Son of God, is the effusion of the Father, truth expressed and manifested infinitely the shining beauty and the splendour of God veiled under the humble flesh of the Son of Man, behind which the Son of God conceals His glory.

But there still remains the sacrifice of the

P

trammels and tyranny of self, and who shall give us the power to make this sacrifice ?

Here we must reckon with the eternal power which controls individuals, families, lands, countries, civilisations.

The Father does not manifest Himself in the conscience alone, but in all the events great and small of our existence and of our world.

The little events are those which affect the little world in which we live, the great are those which trouble a whole country or civilisation. There reign and flourish those great laws of which the secret is in God ; there is also revealed to the observant spectator the work of the Father, making easier for us the sacrifice of ourselves, the abnegation of our individuality, without which there is no faith in Jesus or in His divinity.

There comes a time—I speak of those who live by the mind—when, whether we will it or not, reason is disabused and ceases to believe in its own system.

Perhaps a master has acquired renown by teaching pessimism. When that man has passed his fortieth or fiftieth year, his pessimism becomes a worn-out garment which he cannot even sell. He will not perhaps avow it, but criticism discovers it and cries it out on the house-tops.

When the materialist has arrived at his last hour, you think that, after having wearied those

around him by exalting the virtues of matter and
its intelligent energies, he still regards matter
as the last word which can be spoken. But he
dares no longer affirm this; he is disabused. If
he is not disabused I am sorry for him, for no one
knows what matter is.

You see that our minds are not good for much.
The greatest minds, when they arrive at their full
development, cease to believe in themselves. And
when they are tired, if there were not a disciple
to put new life into the theory and stimulate the
master, how rapidly would the worm-eaten system
from which this master had gained so much
glory crumble away! But the disciple is there.
Help us, he says, one word, master, one page,
prophesy!

Alas! the words are empty, the page is cold,
and the oracles no longer find faith or echo.

And if illusion is obstinate in the conscience of
the man who lives for intellect, he has only to look
to see that mankind is forsaking him. Then an
immense sadness takes hold of him. For what
are glory and the opinion of man? He disdains
them at last as another vanity which passes
away.

Those who live by their hearts are easier to disabuse, because the heart is more easy to touch
than the intellect. The heart is guarded by a few
ribs, and between these ribs there is only a muscle,

which is easy to pierce; while the hide-bound
mind is, like its organ, the brain, enveloped in its
hard and bony case.   It is enclosed in its system
as in a granite fortress, which God alone can
take.

The heart is accessible, especially when it has
loved.   Ardent youth is there to open it; the
illusions of affection at that hour of life move in
rays of light, and envelope the soul with an
enchantment from which few escape.   But when
this intoxication passes, experience quickly shows
us the vanity of its phantoms, the frailty of those
human affections which can only be eternal on
condition that God be in them.   We soon meet
with deceptions which assail the heart like an
open fortress, and then we feel beforehand how
great is the weakness of humanity, and, whether
we will or not—it is the advantage of having
made a few steps in life—we measure the vanity
and the nothingness of all that is earthly.   The
stars which seemed to be our guides on the way
have set, and we find ourselves in the night,
knowing our road no longer; and we ask ourselves what was that light of our life which
has disappeared as all things disappear here
below.

When we see how little is the value in life
of all that is earthly in affection, we do not cling
to it with the same ardour, and thenceforward the

personality which is affected by human love shrinks and becomes poor ; it becomes accustomed to the sacrifice of those vain things which encumber and puff it up.

And the proud, inflated by the vanity of power and riches, how are they broken when a popular movement sweeps away thrones and governments !

It is well for them if they can find a garden in which to plant their cabbages in peace.

Those who had the appearance of wealth and opulence, when the whirlwind of affairs throws them all at once under the car which crushes them, are no longer inflated by their millions.

Providence passes by, and sows on the wind like empty dust the fortune in which they took a pride. We may see it laying low political ambition, which is often the most unwholesome of all the ambitions which spring up in the heart of a man, for it is made of pride and servility.

They seem to be of another race, and will not bow the head, but Providence scatters all. Thus all your systems have grown old, whether sceptical, pantheist, idealist, critical of every kind ; you see to what you are reduced, and how poor a thing was that which took you captive. The teaching of Providence has come to make your sacrifice easy, and free you from your nothingness.

If so, what will you do ? Two ways are open

to you. The way of those who are despairing
and soured, those who shut themselves up in self,
and whom even God cannot subdue, and the way
of those who look up and call upon the Saviour.
On which path will you enter? I will try to
show you how you may enter on that which leads
to salvation.

Jesus spoke the word which contains the
secret of belief : " Repent and believe the Gospel."
He addressed Himself to conscience, because the
conscience plays the preponderant and necessary
part in the act of faith.

Conscience is concerned with the whole man,
since it rules and directs all our actions and
all our faculties ; while the mind constructs its
systems and the heart is concerned with affection,
while ambitious activity is intoxicated with power
and fortune extends its empire, conscience remains
a hidden and deep region wherein is transacted
the great battle between ourselves and God ;
so conscience in the final analysis gives or refuses
faith.

And the word of Jesus is eternally true :
" Repent and believe the Gospel." Every rebellious conscience which does not enter into the
way of repentance, wherein a man recognises
that he is a sinner and beats his breast, will
never arrive at belief. The most invincible
difficulty which we encounter in our priesthood

is not the intellect, though perhaps you think so, not absorbing and tyrannical passion, not fortune or power—no, the terrible difficulty is in the conscience which is closed to repentance. The man who says : " I am an honourable man, I have nothing to reproach myself with," terrifies me ; for who can say with truth : I have nothing to reproach myself with. When you hear that, priest, pass on your way, discussion is useless— there is no place for God in these self-satisfied men.

On the contrary, when you hear a man, whatever he may be, no matter of what age, temperament, culture, human situation—any man, in fact, who is touched by the hand of God and by the warning which you make to him as a priest—when you hear him say : " I don't make myself out better than I am ; I am, like many others, a miserable sinner, but I repent ; " that man, I declare to you, is at the gate of the kingdom of God ; to-morrow he will be on his knees before the Crucified.

All repentant consciences are open to God, who takes possession of them by faith, as all self-satisfied consciences are irremediably closed to Him. Jesus has explained the reason when He said : " Blessed are the poor in spirit, for theirs is the kingdom of God."

Nor does " poor in spirit " mean " fools " ;

the disciples of Jesus often professed humility and gentleness, but never folly.

The poor in spirit are those who consider themselves as poor, stripped of all intellectual, moral, or material riches. To these humble men is reserved the kingdom. Now there are several sorts of riches—common riches, money, worldly wealth. It is easy to hold this as nothing and declare that it is nothing. Mere vile dust! The riches of power which exalt us above others by giving us authority over them; the riches of the mind, more solid than fortune and authority, for it is not like these a good that is borrowed, external to us, but it constitutes our very being; and, finally, the treasure of our affection, more precious than all worldly goods, than all the glory of power and the dazzling gifts of the mind.

Add to these goods the supreme good, virtue, and you have the schedule of the whole wealth of man.

Now, a man poor in spirit as Jesus understood him and sought him as a disciple worthy to enter into His kingdom, is the man who in spirit disdains riches under all these forms, who in his mind has measured the vanity of fortune and of power, who in his mind has known the frailty of those systems, who in his mind has penetrated the nothingness of his love.

But even when you are capable of that you are not yet a moral hero. To be poor in spirit as Jesus willed it, man must have measured before all things the vanity and the nothingness of his own virtue.

When you have realised in yourselves this admirable and heroic poverty—and I beg you to remark all that is grand in this moral doctrine of Jesus and of the Gospel—when you have realised this last poverty and dare not lift your eyes to salvation, you have already stricken your breast, saying: "Lord, have mercy upon me, I am but a publican!" when you have done that, at the first appeal, you will believe in Jesus, Son of God.

Well, I look round me for such souls. I am a priest—that is, one who seeks for souls. I find many poor, not in spirit, but in fact; some are in despair that they have no fortune; others, fallen from power, are in despair to have been cast down yesterday and hope to rise again to-morrow. I find those in despair because of their affections; they tell me their sorrows and show me their wounds still bleeding and not healed over; they are unable to console themselves for being betrayed and abandoned. I find minds disabused of their vain wisdom, but who are overwhelmed with sorrow, and do not look towards the eternal light.

Q

There are few whose wakened consciences say: "I confess I have no virtue, no excellence, no sanctity; I am but a wretch at bottom." They are rare as a precious pearl, they are the predestined, the only ones worthy to enter by faith into the kingdom of God.

The Gospel opens up an excellent road for you to follow. I have revealed it to you in the light of doctrine, of Him whose disciple I am. I have shown you how to become a believer, and I assure you that if you will take that road, faith is at the end of it.

I love to invoke the name of that lost woman, Mary Magdalen, in this place, in this church which is called by her name; she has given us by her example a confirmation of the great manner of believing.

O Mary Magdalen, may thy name penetrate into the heart of women and the conscience of men who listen to me; thou wert, in the life of the Master, a consoling and sublime example; thou didst prove that the woman who is lost—that is to say, whose heart is overwhelmed by passion, which sometimes dishonours and always makes the soul little and narrow—may be born again by faith and trust into the life of God. O Mary Magdalen, make all understand that the way of faith, for those led astray by their mind as well as by their wandering hearts, comes finally to this:

that we must repent and love, recognise our woes and our nothingness, the vanity of all things and of self, to care for nothing but God, who gives eternal life ; in one word, to renounce ourselves and sacrifice all, to open our heart and give ourselves to God.

That is the last word of the Gospel, and it must be the final word also of these conversations which God has permitted us to hold together.

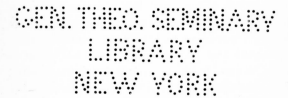

Printed by BALLANTYNE, HANSON *&* CO.
London and Edinburgh